The Worlds of Tomie dePaola

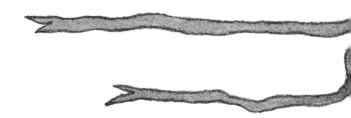

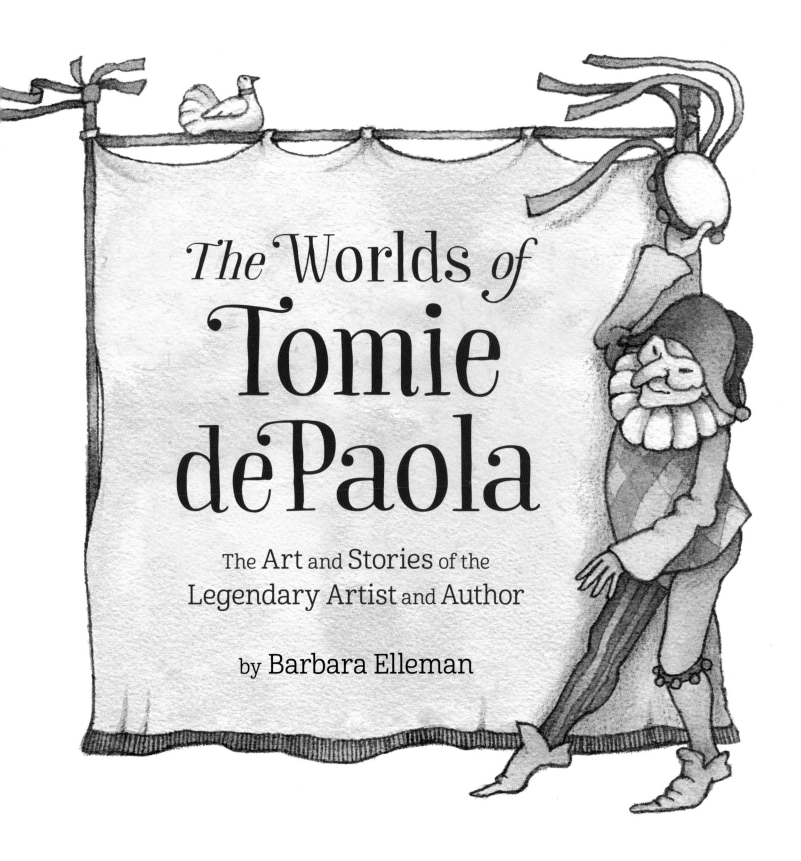

The Worlds of Tomie dePaola

The Art and Stories of the
Legendary Artist and Author

by Barbara Elleman

SIMON & SCHUSTER BOOKS FOR YOUNG READERS
NEW YORK   LONDON   TORONTO   SYDNEY   NEW DELHI

To Don—our time together was never enough

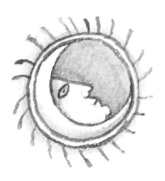

SIMON & SCHUSTER BOOKS FOR YOUNG READERS

An imprint of Simon & Schuster Children's Publishing Division

1230 Avenue of the Americas, New York, New York 10020

Copyright © 1999, 2021 by Barbara Elleman

Previously published in 1999 as *Tomie dePaola: His Art and His Stories*

SIMON & SCHUSTER BOOKS FOR YOUNG READERS is a trademark of Simon & Schuster, Inc.

For information about special discounts for bulk purchases, please contact Simon & Schuster Special Sales
at 1-866-506-1949 or business@simonandschuster.com.

The Simon & Schuster Speakers Bureau can bring authors to your live event. For more information or to book an event,
contact the Simon & Schuster Speakers Bureau at 1-866-248-3049 or visit our website at www.simonspeakers.com.

Jacket design by Laurent Linn. Interior design by Alicia Mikles.

The text of this book was set in Adobe Garamond.

Manufactured in China

1220 SCP

This Simon & Schuster Books for Young Readers hardcover edition March 2021

2 4 6 8 10 9 7 5 3 1

Library of Congress Cataloging-in-Publication Data

Names: Elleman, Barbara author.

Title: The worlds of Tomie dePaola : the art and stories of the legendary artist and author / by Barbara Elleman.

Description: Revised edition. Copyright: 1999, additional material (c) 2021. |

New York : Simon & Schuster Books for Young Readers, 2021. |

Includes bibliographical references and index.

Identifiers: LCCN 2017059000 (print) | LCCN 2018000166 (ebook)

| ISBN 9781534412262 (hardcover : alk. paper) | ISBN 9781534412279 (eBook)

Subjects: LCSH: DePaola, Tomie, 1934– | Authors, American—20th century—Biography. | Illustrators—United States—Biography. |
Children's stories—Authorship. | Illustration of books—United States—20th century.

Classification: LCC PS3554.E1147 (ebook) | LCC PS3554.E1147 Z65 2018 (print) | DDC 813/.54 [B] —dc23

LC record available at https://lccn.loc.gov/2017059000

Contents

Introduction

On March 30, 2020, the hand that gave life to the affable Strega Nona, that infused humor into a book about quicksand, and that brought life to a both poignant and funny childhood incident in *Tom* laid down its brush for the last time. Tomie dePaola, sadly, died suddenly following surgery at Dartmouth-Hitchcock Medical Center near his home in New London, New Hampshire.

Illustrator, artist, author, storyteller. Tomie dePaola intrigued me during my years as a school librarian, as a reviewer and children's book editor at *Booklist*, as editor in chief of *Book Links* for the American Library Association, and in retirement as an active volunteer at the Eric Carle Museum of Picture Book Art.

Through those early years, when an astonishing number of picture books came to my desk for review, Tomie's engrossing stories and accompanying art always struck me as special. His line work, color palettes, and character placements, which added vibrancy to his work, especially challenged me to explore his thought processes and picture book techniques. The result, *Tomie dePaola: His Art and His Stories*, was published in 1999.

Then a couple of years ago, at the nudging of my (and Tomie's) literary agent, Doug Whiteman, I decided to revisit Tomie's career. I read and studied his titles that had stood the test of time, and explored new books that seemingly burst from his ever-creative mind. They offered children—and all readers—imaginative stories filled with distinctive illustrations.

For *The Worlds of Tomie dePaola: The Art and Stories of the Legendary Artist and Author*, as I traced tidbits from our friendship, my understanding of Tomie's innate ability to produce picture books that children love increased. It would be hard to imagine, I mused, the world of children's books without *Strega Nona*, *The Art Lesson*, *"Charlie Needs a Cloak,"* or *The Clown of God*.

I first met Tomie at a conference in Louisville, or maybe it was Atlanta, or possibly Cleveland or Phoenix—neither of us quite remembered or agreed on the actual time or place. Wherever it was, a glass of wine was undoubtedly involved, and there were laughs aplenty. Most important, it marked the beginning of a long, continuing conversation that, in time, involved my husband, who was also a lover of art, theater, and eventually picture books—especially those by Tomie.

Our first meetings, usually in some book-associated situation, typically meandered over which book he was currently working on and what titles were crossing my reviewer's desk. However, as time went on, our conversations became more personal and we began to exchange family stories.

Born in the same year, we both grew up during the Depression and World War II, attended college, found satisfaction in great art (Tomie as artist, I as appreciator), had a proclivity for the theater, and shared a preference for good Italian food.

As we talked, it became obvious that Tomie had a remarkable ability to reach back into his childhood years with clarity, empathy, and an innate understanding of the time. His detail of memory far exceeded mine, and I happily let him entertain me with stories about the up-and-down relationships of grandparents, aunts, uncles, siblings, and cousins who relished one another's foibles and fancies. Thinking back, I hear Tomie's voice and the sound of his ready laughter. I feel the poignancy as he tells the story of his grandmother's death in *Nana Upstairs & Nana Downstairs* or describes the moment he learned about Pearl Harbor in *Here We All Are*, from his 26 Fairmount Avenue series.

At one point in our friendship, we were both scheduled to speak at the University of Southern Mississippi (where Tomie was receiving an award for his total body of work), which triggered conversations of our own college days. Tomie reflected on how Pratt Institute had opened a new world for him—not only solidifying his early determination to become a picture book illustrator, but giving him the opportunity to explore real art in New York museums. He also told of a summer trip to Europe, which gave him the first opportunity to study famous artwork on museum walls instead of just reproductions.

During the years of research for my earlier book, I made several trips to Tomie's home in New London, where he generously opened his files, book archive, personal library, and art collection to my scrutiny. He made time for formal interviews as well as impromptu chats, where our conversations often centered on the art of the picture book. Over time we discussed, dissected, and sometimes squabbled over narrative flow, the constriction of the gutter, the art of the gap, and the turn of the page. Tomie had definite ideas, as did I, about what makes a picture book work—and neither of us minced words when defining them.

One day our talks turned to religion. He suggested that instead of discussion, I look at a couple of his picture books. I chose *The Clown of God* and then paged through *Francis, the Poor Man of Assisi*, where his choice of color often gives sign to his feelings. However, in *Days of the Blackbird* his placement and movement of the characters, especially the birds, best echo Tomie's deep connections to his faith.

On another occasion we talked theater—a topic that intrigued us both. He regaled me with stories of his dancing days, the variety shows he choreographed, his teaching drama at Colby-Sawyer College, and his work backstage in summer theater. Tomie's keen sense of planning for a stage performance was complementary to laying out pages for a picture book. As he suggested, "An illustrator casts the play, costumes the characters, plans entrances and exits, designs the set, and moves the action forward while not losing sight of the overall plot." And I agreed!

One of our last conversations centered on when *The Worlds of Tomie dePaola: The Art and Stories of the Legendary Artist and Author* would go to press. While proud, happy, and delighted with the jacket, he had no comments about the text. That, he said laughingly, was up to me. So . . .

Fare thee well, Tomie.

A Tribute to Tomie

Once upon a time in the 1970s, for some now forgotten reason, I decided to do an illustration in the style of Tomie dePaola. A clever forgery was actually what I was after, and I clearly remember thinking that it would take ten or twenty minutes of my time, tops. I'd always had a knack for imitating different drawings and handwriting styles, and I was sure I could knock off a "Tomie" drawing as easy as pie for the book jacket or a birthday card or whatever it was I was doing.

I sat down at my drawing table with the three-hundred-pound Fabriano watercolor paper, the stacks of colored pencils, the best watercolors, and all the art supplies that I knew Tomie was fond of using. Six hours later, sweaty, frustrated, and thoroughly puzzled, I tore up the thirty-eighth ruined piece of paper in despair. No matter how hard I tried—in fact, the harder I tried—the further I got from success; I could not imitate Tomie's way of drawing. That seemingly formulaic style, with its simple line, its folksy composition, and its childlike color, was a lot more complex and sophisticated than I had bargained for—and almost impossible to duplicate in spirit.

Like almost everyone else, I was looking at the surface of things and making the wrong assumption. I'd forgotten about the old standard myth that also happens to be true: the artist always draws or paints him- or herself, no matter what the subject and no matter what or how the approach. We illustrators create and re-create ourselves over and over—not just in the ways our unwitting pens and brushes draw sets of features that look much more like ourselves than, say, the enchanted frog, but in the very atmosphere, tone, and approach we lay down for a story. You can tell a whole lot about an illustrator's spirit and personal stuff from his or her illustrations.

Tomie's illustrations are just like Tomie: They look easy but they're not. He's a puzzle and an enigma. He's also a lot of fun and hard to ignore. I've been Tomie's friend for almost twenty-five years, and I am still not sure who he is. I have come to think of him as a force of nature: comforting, playful, and nurturing sometimes; stormy, scornful, and angry at other times. And sometimes he's just not there! He travels around the whole world like Old Mother West Wind or the North Wind in Norse fairy tales—here today, gone tomorrow. I call Tomie to ask a question and get his assistant, Bob. "So, hey, Bob, how ya doing? Where's Tomie?" Bob says, "In Australia." Wow! Here one day, gone the next!

Nevertheless, when Tomie and I get together, it's usually a happy place to be. Tomie can laugh and be silly and carry on like nobody else in this world. Tomie's house and gardens are always beautiful, stunning, and the most fantastic place you can visit in this part of the New England landscape.

I always think that Tomie's house should be transplanted to New Mexico. I can't understand why he lives in New Hampshire, except that that's just the other part of Tomie—he won't ever give up. He's strong, stubborn, witty, and tough. He's Irish! He's Italian! He's gone before you know it, and there when you think he's gone. He's our hero; a Connecticut Yankee disguised as Mother Goose. Everybody loves Tomie because his books are basically loved, needed, and meaningful. They're a lot of fun, and hard to ignore; playful, thoughtful, enigmatic, and impossible to imitate (maybe he uses a magic crayon). He's a well-crafted legend and a searching, grown-up child. And all of that with such ease and joy and confidence. *Viva Tomie!*

Trina Schart Hyman
LYME, NH
JUNE 1998

"I use my garden like I use my paints."

1

A Life

Stepping into Tomie dePaola's home is much like walking into the pages of his books. While one is subliminally aware of the thoughtfully controlled design, the eye focuses on the feast of color, the array of art objects both solemn and amusing, and the surprising details that promise a story. At one time three life-size, fleece-covered mountain goats stood in the entryway. But what still permeates both house and book is an abiding warmth and conviviality.

Without a doubt dePaola's New London, New Hampshire, home was an artistic experience, but the human factor—his large, welcoming smile; the rush of his laugh; his exuberant greeting—is what is most memorable. His enthusiasm carried across the threshold and provided an easy cushion for free-flowing, pithy conversations about art, illustration, books, writing, folklore, research, travel, family, and life in general. In the background classical music would filter through the rooms, while outside, his wooden deck, stretching lawn, and lavish flower beds melded into the ambience. And even when dePaola traveled, the place echoed with his effervescent personality. Yet one could sense that beneath dePaola's ebullience lay a highly complicated man with a private place that he reserved for himself, that his home was not a showcase for admirers but integral to his own artistic expression.

The large, airy rooms, which provide an apt setting for dePaola's diverse array of folklore objects, inevitably lead to the kitchen, where a crowd of cookbooks, copper pots and pans, and gleaming bowls answered his gourmet inclinations. Seven ovens—from high-tech microwave to beehive brick—attest to his cooking skills. To dine in dePaola's home was a culinary experience not to be forgotten.

Across a brick and plant-filled patio, a renovated barn houses his studio and Whitebird, Incorporated, the business side of dePaola's enterprises. Here the precise layout found in the house still gives way to working clutter.

DePaola paintings provide centerpieces for comfortable folk-art-filled rooms.

Telephones ring and computers still hum under the direction of a continuing assistant. An immense collection of DVDs shares space with pieces of dePaola's framed art, while boxes of letters from children, packets of publicity brochures, and cartons of new books vie for space on the floor and tables. Here and there a stuffed Mother Goose, a Big Anthony puppet, and a cardboard Bill and Pete (various commercial and child-made versions sent by admirers) continue to reflect the broader aspects of today's children's book business.

DePaola's office.

While once the barn's loft held copies of dePaola's more than 270 titles (including numerous foreign editions), today much of this collection is housed at the University of Connecticut, along with hundreds of pieces of original illustrations and paintings, large and small. When asked whether or not the paintings were "fine art" pieces destined for museum exhibitions, dePaola had replied, "I call these my 'non-book' art, so as not to belittle the illustrations I do for books."

On the first floor of the barn, a connecting door leads to dePaola's private studio. While stacks of books in the house reflect his multisided reading tastes (everything from fiction and biography to filmography), here the walls are lined with reference books on art, illustration, folklore, and other titles helpful to his work. In the center of the room stands a large drawing board surrounded by tubes of paint, colored pencils, brushes wide and narrow (dePaola called them his household gods), bottles of water, and bits of paper cluttered with the illustrator's visual thoughts. A high stool (still claiming its original paint) from his art school days stands nearby. Along the walls are childhood photos and early drawings, a daily reminder of the boy dePaola once was—and in memory still is today.

For what gave dePaola so much credibility with children has roots in his own life, beginning with his childhood. Born on September 15, 1934, in Meriden, Connecticut, dePaola was named Thomas Anthony after his two grandfathers— Tom Downey, his Irish grandfather, who owned a combination grocery and

DePaola in his studio.

butcher store, and Antonio dePaola, his Italian grandfather, who died many years before dePaola was born.

His paternal grandparents, Concetta and Antonio, came from Calabria, a region in southern Italy, which the artist turned into the setting of *Strega Nona*. His mother's ancestors emigrated from Ireland and England. Charles Parkin Mock, after arriving in the United States from Devonshire, found a job as farm foreman on an estate near New Haven, Connecticut, where he soon met and married the cook, Honorah O'Rourke, recently arrived from County Cork, Ireland. One of their three children, Mary Alice, married Thomas Lawrence Downey, also of Irish ancestry; their

The Italian grandparents: Concetta (Nana Fall-River) and Antonio dePaola (before 1919).

The Irish grandparents: Tom and Mary Alice (Nana Downstairs) Downey (1955).

only daughter, Florence, known to the family as Flossie, met a man named Joseph dePaola at a dance. Florence and Joseph's marriage in 1929 produced four children, the second of whom was Tomie.

This large, intimate, fun-loving Irish-Italian mix of people, dePaola would proclaim, "loved telling old tales on each other; laughter and storytelling was an everyday ingredient. My parents had such a joy of life." DePaola drew on this family joie de vivre in his depictions of the up-and-down relationships of his grandparents, aunts and uncles, siblings, and cousins—not in a tell-all, finger-pointing fashion but in the warmhearted tradition of a close extended family that relishes one another's fancies and foibles.

As a young boy dePaola often felt overshadowed by his older brother, Joe. Buddy, as Joe was called, was born four years earlier and had, according to dePaola, completely won the hearts of the entire dePaola and Downey families. "Although my mother tried to persuade everyone that I was a positive addition, the turmoil I created with my lungs didn't convince anyone."[1] Early animosities between the brothers continued through the years, and the two were never close; Joe died young, in his early forties, but dePaola's edgy relationship with his brother always struck a raw chord.

DePaola's parents: Florence (Flossie) and Joe dePaola (1928).

His youngest sister, Judie, grew up mostly after dePaola left home; their age difference resulted in fewer family memories in common. With his sister Maureen, whose birth is chronicled in *The Baby Sister*, dePaola shared puppet making as children and partnering in ballet performances as teenagers. While dePaola himself had no children, his siblings have ensured the continuity of the family line with nine nieces and nephews, who in turn have produced children of their own.

DePaola grew up in the difficult years of the Depression, when money was tight for a family whose only income producer was a barber. Even then, books were important. When dePaola was a toddler, his mother read to him, and his family encouraged his early artistic attempts. He once recalled the excitement of getting a box of Crayola

The dePaola family: Joe Jr. (Buddy), Judie, Maureen, Tomie, Flossie, and Joe (mid-1940s).

crayons that contained one the color of his skin. "With one stroke I could accomplish what none of the other forty-seven colors combined allowed me to do: fill in a human face and make it look like me."[2] And he joyfully remembered his ninth Christmas, when all his presents were art supplies—the greatest pleasure being an easel. As his mother once said, "He took to reading at a very young age, and he always had a pencil in his hand. I remember him coming home from kindergarten one day and telling me he was going to draw pictures for books, dance and sing on stage, and paint all the scenery."[3]

DePaola's early interest in art was, in fact, equaled by his love of theater. When his father built him a sandbox, he turned it over and used it as a stage. Puppet shows and backyard "extravaganzas" were performed over the years, and his tap-dancing

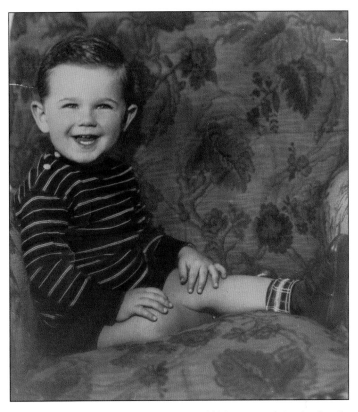

A beaming two-year-old Tomie poses in the family wing chair, which, years later, becomes the prototype for the chair found in several scenes in *The Baby Sister*.

lessons, which started at age five, continued until he entered art school in 1952. He and his friend Carol Morrissey danced their way through numerous local benefits and shows, even performing once in New York City. Years later, at dePaola's sixtieth birthday party (shared with four hundred of his "closest friends"), Morrissey and dePaola re-created their "Once in Love with Amy" routine, to the delight of all the partygoers. The dancers never missed a beat!

Tomie's father, a home-movie buff, captured many family events with his eight-millimeter camera. Relatives and neighbors found themselves on film celebrating birthdays, relishing the Sunday funnies, eating spaghetti, decorating for Christmas, and enjoying other family happenings. One of the most significant was when the family built their own house—at 26 Fairmount Avenue. During the construction process the young budding artist found hundreds of feet of blank walls at his disposal. With a piece of blue carpenter's chalk, he created "murals" of the family on the plasterboard. Proud of his handiwork, dePaola said he was devastated when the workers covered the walls with paint. He also drew pictures on the bedsheets at night before going to sleep, using a penlight to guide his busy hand. Or at least he did, dePaola remembered, "until my mother stopped me."

DePaola admits to being a difficult child, partly because, he said, "I was willful and outspoken." He determinedly experimented in the kitchen. "I found out that flour and water and ketchup, deep fried, didn't taste very good, but I had to discover that for myself." In second grade he was unable to see any reason to learn his arithmetic tables. "I, who could sing any song after hearing it once, memorize any poem, tell the plot of any movie I had seen, could not memorize my tables. As I told my teacher, I was not going to be an 'arithmetic-er'; I was going to be an artist. Furthermore, I thought it was a real waste of white paper."

Mrs. Beulah Bowers, an early art teacher who features in dePaola's book *The Art Lesson*, was more understanding of dePaola's artistic temperament; she supported his early endeavors, and the two became fast friends. In fourth grade, confident of his talent, dePaola sent a drawing to Walt Disney and was thrilled, but not surprised, to receive an answer. Mr. Disney returned the drawing, saying how important it was for artists to "keep their early work," and suggesting that dePaola "continue to practice." Unfortunately, the art piece and the letter have been lost in a lifetime of moves. However, dePaola recalled, those words made such an impression on him that still today he takes his letters to children seriously, realizing the impact they can have on a child.

High school, dePaola remembered, was "full and wonderful." And while academics were never a problem, he admitted that "for a 'non-arithmetic-er,' algebra was tough" and that "missing the first two weeks of my freshman year because of illness didn't help." Not surprisingly, Art Club and Props and Paints (the drama club) took much of his time, and his dancing talents earned him the title of resident choreographer for the annual variety shows and Christmas programs. To everyone's delight, he usually turned up on the stage as well. A plum, but not unexpected, assignment came in his senior year, when he was named art editor of the school yearbook.[4]

Something else he remembered from those teen years would, unknown to him at the time, have future implications. In what became a Friday-night ritual in the dePaola home, family friends gathered around the television set to

DePaola's rendering in *The Art Lesson* of his beloved art teacher, Mrs. Beulah Bowers.

watch the fights, popular fare in the 1950s. One of the visitors, Florence Nesci, introduced the teenage dePaola to the fine art of making popcorn—a treat he has been "hooked on ever since" and that was the inspiration for his writing and illustrating *The Popcorn Book* some twenty years later.[5] A large commercial-style popcorn maker, showing

DePaola partners sister Maureen
for a ballet performance.

High-stepping dePaola dances
the Charleston with a friend
for a Pratt Institute benefit.

signs of much use, still stands in dePaola's barn today.

Talking with dePaola about his childhood and teen years quickly revealed that the important events in his life, and his memories of them, inevitably channeled into—and sometimes overlapped in—four areas: family, art, theater, and religion.

A case in point is his choice of art school. His mother's twin cousins, Franny and Fuffy McLaughlin, had studied at Pratt Institute in Brooklyn; by the early 1940s they had established themselves as top-notch photographers

DePaola's dancing feet find their way into *Oliver Button Is a Sissy*.

in the magazine field.[6] DePaola also chose Pratt, a decision he attributed to the twins' influence; winning a highly competitive two-thousand-dollar scholarship given by the city of Meriden made going to art school possible. Life at Pratt opened a new world for dePaola; the concentration of classes in art (except for one English class) for eight hours a day, five days a week, shaped his way of working for the rest of his life. "My four years at Pratt," he related, "were heaven on earth. We had working artists who gave us our specialty courses, and then a wonderful core faculty who taught us how to draw. Observe and practice, we were told, observe and practice. Keep your eyes open and draw, draw, draw."

The "us" he referred to included now familiar names in the children's book field. DePaola shared classes and inspiration with Anita and Arnold Lobel, Ted Lewin, Charles Mikolaycak, Cyndy Szekeres, and John Schoenherr.[7] The paths of these seven people would cross many times through the years as their expertise and reputations grew in the children's literature field. But getting there wasn't always easy. DePaola lived in a small one-room apartment on Washington Street in Brooklyn, using half the space for his studio. "I had funds one month to buy some watercolor paints and a box of cornflakes, and another month to get a piece of meat and good paper," dePaola laughingly remembered. He also recalls the need to save his money in order to buy Ruth Krauss and Maurice Sendak's then newly published *A Hole Is to Dig*, which he found "highly inventive." However, for his own developing tastes

the introduction to the folkloric style—the simple lines, carefully composed shapes, and flat perspective—of Alice and Martin Provensen had a stronger impact.[8]

Brooklyn gave dePaola easy access to New York's many museums. It was at the Museum of Modern Art, for instance, where he indulged his love of old films, especially silent ones. Perhaps it was the combination of film and art that spurred dePaola's interest in sequence illustration, a technique he effectively uses in many of his books.[9] And in what became a turning point in his artistic outlook, he attended a show featuring the work of the French expressionist Georges Rouault, whose de-sentimentalization of religious art would be a great influence.[10] "That changed my point of view. I realized that art was something more than I had thought, and I opened myself

Children's illustrator Anita Lobel poses with her portrait, painted by dePaola during their Pratt art school days.

up to its influences, not so much from the aspect of illustration or commercial art but from what the fine artists were doing."

It was also during this time that he became acquainted with the work of Ben Shahn.[11] In 1955, while spending a summer studying fresco and painting at the Skowhegan School of Painting and Sculpture, dePaola met Shahn, who for a time became his mentor.[12] He remembered Shahn once telling him, "Being an artist is not only what you *do* with your artwork but how you live your life."[13] In his autobiography, *Between Worlds*, Leo Lionni, who also names Shahn as a mentor, says, "Shahn was fundamentally a storyteller— his paintings always refer the beholder to an event."[14] With this in mind, it is easy to see why dePaola felt a connection to Shahn's work. One need only look, for instance, at Shahn's children's book *Ounce, Dice, Trice* to see a similarity of strong line and fluidity of pen stroke.

DePaola presents *Still Life with Fruit*, completed for an assignment at Pratt.

DePaola's interest in fresco derived from his growing passion for contemporary liturgical art, which, in turn, had such an impact on his life and thoughts that in his junior year at Pratt he considered leaving art school to join a monastery. Dissuaded by classmates and by Mother Placid, an artist who lived in a Benedictine monastery for women in Connecticut and who became a guiding friend,[15] he finished Pratt and, as a gift from his parents, spent a summer in Europe. "Seeing all those beautiful pieces of art that I had seen only in the pages of art-history books," dePaola remembered, "was wondrous."

The tour of Europe took an amazing turn. The ship dePaola and his friends sailed on was the *Andrea Doria*, which, a week after they disembarked, collided with the *Stockholm* on its return journey to America and sank into the sea. Years later the

Andrea Doria's resting place was found and its safe retrieved from the watery depths. In a follow-up television documentary, a traveler's check from the safe was shown.[16] On the check, written in India ink and as clear as on the day it was written, was the signature "Thomas dePaola."[17]

When dePaola returned from abroad, the urge to join a small monastery had not diminished, and in 1956 he made a commitment to a priory in Vermont.[18] He stayed for six months, left, returned, and left again. "I was meant to be an illustrator and writer of children's books, which was clear to me as a child, and seems clear now, but those on-and-off monastery years were an unsettling time in my life. While I still dreamed of becoming a children's book illustrator, I didn't know how to make that happen. I was living in Vermont, all the publishers were in New York, and in those days editors and art directors wanted people who were close at hand."

He hadn't stopped drawing, however. He designed Christmas cards for the Katherine Crockett Company in Vermont, produced items for a craftsmen's guild, worked in summer theater as a set designer, and even performed in several plays. And neither had he forsaken his interest in liturgical art. For the next years his artistic endeavors revolved around creating murals and church vestments. DePaola calls this phase his "Brief Period." He was "briefly in a monastery, briefly lived in France, briefly designed church vestments, and was even briefly married."[19] Traces of his religious art training can be found in the backgrounds of books such as *Francis, the Poor Man of Assisi*; *The Lady of Guadalupe*; *The Parables of Jesus*; and *The Clown of God*. Although most of his murals have been dismantled or painted over in the course of redecoration, several can still be found in the Glastonbury Abbey in Hingham, Massachusetts,[20] and at the Dominican Retreat and Conference Center in Niskayuna, New York.[21]

These years could also be called dePaola's "Restless Period." Following his brief time in Paris, he went to Boston to teach art at Newton College of the Sacred Heart; relocated to San Francisco, where he was named assistant professor of art at Lone

DePaola's spirituality ran deep throughout his life, as evidenced by this delicate figure of Mary that graces one of the wall niches in his studio.

DePaola spent the late 1950s and early 1960s creating liturgical murals, this one in 1960 for Saint Sylvester Church in Graniteville, Vermont. Entitled *Christ's Entry into Jerusalem*, the piece was rendered in acrylic on wood and was five by twelve feet in dimension.

Mountain College, and where he received his master of fine arts at the California College of Arts and Crafts; returned to Boston as instructor of art at Chamberlayne Junior College; and then moved to New Hampshire, where he held first the position of designer and technical director in speech and theater at Colby-Sawyer College, then that of associate professor of art at New England College, and later was named artist-in-residence at New England College.[22]

Brought up Catholic, dePaola had found early delight in the church's mysteries, liturgies of worship, and stories of saints. "Once, when I was ten, I stayed for three continuous showings of the movie *The Song of Bernadette*. I was so transfixed by Bernadette's pure and simple faith that I would probably still be there if my worried parents hadn't tracked me down." As an adult he had grown away from the church. Although, he said, spirituality had always been a driving force in his life.

In San Francisco, group therapy sessions allowed dePaola to get in touch with his inner child. For some time he had felt his career as an illustrator was reaching an impasse; his work, he feared, was becoming unimaginative, uncreative, as colorless as the fog outside his San Francisco window. "I had totally fallen for that old line 'Don't be childish,' and I had smothered my childlikeness; I had to like that child again." In particular dePaola credits a therapist who agreed to take her fee in paintings, and through them she helped him once again discover the childlike pleasure in his art—the intensity—that he had had as a youngster.

In addition he found his Whitebird symbol. A priest friend was coming to dePaola's apartment for a "home liturgy" celebration for Pentecost, the feast of the Holy Spirit.[23] Each person attending was asked to contribute a poem or a song. DePaola said he chose a piece of music called "White Bird" because the white bird is the symbol of the Holy Spirit.[24] "I realized that white birds had shown up in my work, and I remembered that in mythology the white bird was the messenger between the gods and humans. I know I get my inspiration from a higher source, and what better  symbol for an artist, especially for me?" Nestled in windows, flapping from eaves, the white bird symbol continued to show up in his books. "It's my way," dePaola said, "of acknowledging the source of my talent."

Nowhere, perhaps, do white birds play a greater role than in dePaola's Christmas celebrations. The artist's love of the holiday is well known; he holds the season "in quiet awe as a time for contemplating life's mysteries and wonders."[25] In early December, Christmas folk-art pieces, tiny lights, fragrant greens, votive candles, and Christmas cactus, poinsettia, and amaryllis plants filled the house.

The bold colors of Christmas offer striking contrast to the white walls in dePaola's home, which, he claimed, become a perfect canvas. He traced his love of Christmas back to his childhood. "I was three or four, and we still lived in a rented apartment. My father had a make-believe fireplace. I can still see it—covered with red crepe paper, with a fake log and a red electric light bulb. 'That's where Santa comes,' my father told me. When we moved to Fairmount Avenue, we had a real chimney and real fireplace. My father put blue lights in all the windows. I was very impressed. During World War II we had blackouts and had to be careful of using lights, but when peace came and we could once more put lights in every window at Christmastime, I was delighted. When I got older, I created a life-size Nativity set on our lawn. Every year I added more carolers, choirboys, angels, all the way through art school."

Even after he left home and didn't have much money, dePaola found inexpensive ways to decorate for Christmas. "I read that in medieval times people decorated with roses and apples, so I made hundreds of tissue-paper roses, some of which I still have. . . . Years ago, I read something that said Christmas is when 'the invisible becomes visible,' and I thought that was a wonderful thing to say about Christmas— as well as something for an artist to keep in mind. Those words have stayed with me through the years."[26]

In 1962, while teaching at Newton College of the Sacred Heart, dePaola garnered good reviews for his several one-man shows at Boston's the Botolph Group, a gallery that featured his contemporary religious art.[27] This early acclaim might have

At Christmastime, folk-art pieces, candles, and poinsettias intermingle, bringing a delight of color to dePaola's home.

led him on an entirely different career path. However, his desire to become an illustrator had not gone away, and he decided to work out his teaching schedule so that he could live in New York—and be closer to the publishing community.

Through a series of coincidences, dePaola met Florence Alexander, an art representative, who became his agent and an influential force in his professional life.[28] "Florence," dePaola said, "created my career for me. She made me work very hard and take all kinds of funny little jobs and get my name out there. I owe a tremendous amount to her."[29] When then Coward-McCann editor in chief Alice Torrey decided to publish a physical science series for young readers using a visual picture-book approach, she hired Bernice Kohn (later known as Bernice Hunt) as the series editor.[30] It was Kohn's idea to launch the series with two books, one by a known artist and one by a new talent. She went to Alexander's office looking for an unknown illustrator; Alexander recommended dePaola. After perusing his portfolio, Kohn signed him up to illustrate *Sound*, which she herself had written under the pseudonym Lisa Miller. Later that year dePaola also illustrated *Wheels*, the third book in a loosely grouped series.

DePaola and his mother—in a mock depiction of Grant Wood's *American Gothic*, 1979.

Following his return from San Francisco and his breakthrough to "the child within," as dePaola called it, his books rolled off the presses in quick succession. He illustrated eight books in 1973, four of which he wrote, including *Nana Upstairs & Nana Downstairs* and *"Charlie Needs a Cloak."* In 1974 he could count three finished publications; there were six in 1975, and nine in 1976. The banner year was surely 1977. DePaola produced artwork for fourteen titles, three that he wrote himself. At long last his dream of being a children's book illustrator was coming true. While reviewers hailed him as a "new talent" on the children's book scene, for dePaola it was the culmination of long, hard years of trying to get a foothold in the children's publishing world. These vividly remembered frustrations are one of the reasons why dePaola so treasured his home and his Whitebird barn and studio.

Over the years dePaola began to realize just how important it was for him—and for his artistic creativity—to inhabit a living space that made him feel joyful. Inspired by his love of color, space, and light, he enlarged his house and expanded his already bountiful gardens. As he continued to add to his folk-art and primitive collections, the need for even more space became clear. In 2004 a large addition resulted in what he called the Mercer Room, named after a small boutique hotel in SoHo, in Manhattan, where large spaces and natural light attract a variety of artists. Nearly fourteen hundred square feet, the Mercer Room has a high ceiling and huge windows that overlook his garden. The walls feature vibrant paintings, some of which dePaola created, with niches containing clay figurines, candles, bird sculptures, and other folk-art objects representing places where dePaola had gone and people he had known throughout the world. Friends have called these displays "Tomie's Collections." In a feature in *New Hampshire Home* magazine (November/December 2014), dePaola commented that his home was a "dream come true; a place I love and that inspires my art." The writer of the piece, Andi Axman, noted in amazement that "his house could easily be mistaken for a folk art gallery."[31]

Across the patio, the collections continue in his barn and studio; more niches filled with art pieces line the walls. In a far corner a chair draped with a Mexican serape provides a quiet space for morning meditations. Library shelves hold hundreds of books that helped dePaola with research projects. The collection focuses on titles about art and illustration, biographies about others working in the illustration field, and books about fine artists he admired, such as Matisse, Giotto, Fra Angelico, and Hockney.

Further proof of his creative expertise flourishes in the many children's literature awards that dePaola had garnered through the years. One of the earliest was a 1976 Caldecott Honor Award for *Strega Nona*, a book that became a turning point in his career. Then, in 2000, *26 Fairmount Avenue* received a Newbery Honor Award for distinguished writing. Having long felt unsure of his ability to produce a cohesive

The covers of dePaola's first informational books depict his early sense of design, penchant for whimsy, and ability to connect with children.

Through the anteroom, one enters the Mercer Room—named after a boutique hotel in New York City—which overlooks dePaola's beautiful garden.

A folk-art skull adorns the library in dePaola's studio.

story that reflected his own life and people he loved, dePaola found sweet confirmation in this honor. When in 2011 the American Library Association presented dePaola with the prestigious Children's Literature Legacy Award (known at the time as the Laura Ingalls Wilder Award), given for a substantial and lasting contribution to literature for children, his joy overflowed. (See the appendix for a full list of awards and recognition.)

As his own career expanded and critical acclaim continued, and being cognizant of the various ways that others had helped him, dePaola developed a close relationship with the Society of Children's Book Writers and Illustrators. He became fast friends with organizers Lin Oliver and Stephen Mooser. For several years dePaola served on their board of advisors, and he was instrumental in their adding the *I* to SCBWI. He regularly participated in the society's meetings—conducting the first master class at a conference, founding an annual Tomie dePaola Illustrator Award for promising new talent, and producing a master-class video for their DVD series.

Early in his career, looking for a place where his work could be secure and yet available for study, dePaola met with Karen Hoyle, the then director of the Kerlan Collection at the University of Minnesota. He donated his work to their archives so that others could examine, for example, early versions of *Strega Nona*, or Charlie from *"Charlie Needs a Cloak."* Later, deciding that the University of Connecticut—his home state—offered the advantages of being nearer to where he lived and worked, and also having a more sophisticated storage and tracking system, he decided to place his future work in their Northeast Children's Literature Collection.

Though success no longer eluded him, its extent, he admitted, often baffled him. When asked to comment about the deeper meanings of his stories, the usually exuberant and rarely shy dePaola said that he found it difficult to discuss the intricacies of his own work. He preferred the format through which he "talks" with children: the words and images on the page.

DePaola's dedication for *Quiet* reads, "For all those who know the beauty of QUIET—and pass it on to others."

DePaola drawing at his light table.

2

Autobiographical Tales

On a television in dePaola's studio, pictures from old family movies often flickered across the screen, bringing images of the artist-author's family to life. His father, an ardent photographer and also a home-movie buff, rarely let a birthday party, summer picnic at the beach, Christmas festivity, or any other family gathering go by without recording it on film. The great-grandparents, grandparents, parents, siblings, and other relatives who once so readily posed for the senior dePaola's camera now inhabit his son's stories, radiating warmth and believability.

DePaola, the recipient of these family treasures, said that these old home movies provided him with laughs and memories; it is obvious that they also furnished inspirational grist for his ever-active creative mind. Evidence of the films' and photos' influence crops up in his books in several ways. In *Nana Upstairs & Nana Downstairs* the protagonist's father is seen in the background with a home movie camera; in *Tom* and in *The Baby Sister*, photographic-style drawings identify the characters; and in *The Art Lesson* his photographer cousins make a cameo appearance. In a more general manner his father's old movies reconnected dePaola with his past and acted as a memory check for the background details that give such warm ambience to his illustrations. And while the artist had an acute recollection about events of his childhood, viewing these

Oliver Button Is a Sissy.

The title page arrangement, an example of dePaola's early sense of design, places Andy atop the letters *A-N-D-Y*. The author's name, as though being announced by the boy, is seen in a balloon over Andy's head, while the subtitle, "That's My Name," appears in parentheses beneath the large letters. DePaola traces the idea to a graphic treatment he once saw used in an old film title.

Told entirely through maroon-and-brown-shaded pictures and clever dialogue balloons, the story follows young Andy as he carts the letters of his name to a group of older children, in the hope of joining their play. Instead they grab the letters and make a variety of words, shutting him out of their fun. A disgruntled Andy finally gathers his courage and his letters, saying, "I may be little, but I'm very important," and leaves. The final spread, echoing the title page, finds him on top of the letters, curled up protectively around his name, fast asleep. Humor, as well as an understanding of a child's feelings, makes this deceptively simple concept book an excellent choice to share with children today.

Published later that same year, *Nana Upstairs & Nana Downstairs* has a direct connection to dePaola's life and is his first truly autobiographical book. In the story young Tommy eagerly visits his grandmother (Nana Downstairs) and his feeble great-grandmother (Nana Upstairs), who is confined to her bed on the second floor. He happily watches Nana Downstairs bake a cake and comb Nana Upstairs's long, white hair into a bun, and then lovingly shares candy mints and stories with her.

The real Nana Downstairs and Nana Upstairs, clipped from an old home movie.

When Nana Upstairs dies, Tommy is devastated. Comfort arrives in the form of a falling star that Tommy witnesses late one night; his mother tells him, "Perhaps that

Nana Downstairs with young Tomie.

was a kiss from Nana Upstairs." The final page reveals a grown-up Tommy remembering Nana Downstairs, also now deceased. Seeing another falling star, he thinks, *Now you are both Nana Upstairs.* The well-conceived ending is an endearing tribute to his two nanas, from both the real Tomie and his fictional counterpart. This fast-forward-to-the-future technique, one dePaola also nimbly employs in *The Art Lesson*, gives readers a glimpse of dePaola as an adult and sends a message about growing older and the cycles of life.

To give artistic balance to both the sad and the uplifting aspects of the two nanas' story, dePaola chose subdued hues of umber and rose, highlighted with black lines and soft shading. The framing of each page with a scrolled design evokes old scalloped-edged photographs of the 1930s and results in a harmonious connection between pictures and story, which no doubt has contributed to the book's early and continued popularity.

A sign of the meaningful message of *Nana Upstairs & Nana Downstairs* to readers and to dePaola was the re-release of the title in 1998, for the book's twenty-fifth anniversary. Considered to be pivotal to his autobiographical body of work, *Nana* was given a trim size similar to that of *The Art Lesson*, *The Baby Sister*, and *Tom*, and was reillustrated in full color.

The same scene from the 1973 and 1998 editions of *Nana Upstairs & Nana Downstairs* display the differences in line and color.

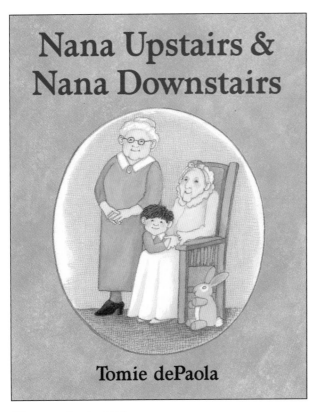

The cover for the 1998 edition of *Nana Upstairs & Nana Downstairs*.

When he began to update his drawings in preparation for the color, dePaola found that he needed to alter his line work as well, which provided a unique opportunity and a great challenge. As dePaola notes in the book's afterword, "It was not easy to re-illustrate the book in full color. It was hardly a matter of 'colorizing' or coloring in. My drawing style has changed subtly over time, so twenty-five years later I have approached *Nana Upstairs & Nana Downstairs* as a completely new book. It was important for me to retain the nostalgic feeling of the original, and I did this mostly with the use of soft color. Creating this art was as emotional an experience for me now as it was then." His efforts, especially the way the gentle new colors retain the original atmosphere, have been successful; in updating the art, he lost none of the story's sensitivity.

In the new illustrations the artist's subtle changes bring more intimacy to the pictures. For example, backgrounds are texturized, pushing the images forward; the furniture is given a smooth shine, making the pictures less busy; and the characters' expressions are refined. An interesting connection can be found in the use of a large, teal-colored wing chair where Tommy is told of Nana Upstairs's death; undoubtedly, it is the same one that plays a role in *The Baby Sister*. The book's original cover art was moved to the back of the jacket. Then a clever manipulation of graphics happened. An interior image from the earlier edition shows Tommy's father making a home movie, with Tommy's brother, Buddy, holding the light. The camera focuses on Tommy and his two nanas. This threesome, enlarged and set in a cameo-shaped frame, warmly graces the front of the book's dust jacket.

Another family allusion worth noting is a reference to his grandfather Tom, whom dePaola has featured in two different books: *Now One Foot, Now the Other*, published in 1981, which actually takes place after the incident described in *Tom*, published twelve years later, in 1993.

When dePaola was a child, he and his Irish grandfather enjoyed a special relationship, which is clearly apparent in both titles. In *Now One Foot, Now the Other* the young protagonist is Bobby, and his grandfather is Bob—a more elderly and much feebler man than he is in *Tom*—and dePaola and his grandfather's real-life closeness shines through the fictional framework. Bob encourages toddler Bobby to walk by telling him, "Now one foot, now the other," a message that Bobby repeats some years later to his grandfather when he needs to relearn to walk after suffering from a stroke.

DePaola effectively ties the alternating situations (the old helping the young, the young helping the old) together through a simple game of playing blocks. When described the first time the game is a straightforward part of the story line; later it becomes a poignant memory that helps Bob on his road to recovery. Throughout the book dePaola places the characters up front on the page and limits background detail, giving drama to his portrayals. Again, color is put to good use, drawing viewers through the well-thought-out perspectives. The repeated images of Bob and Bobby at various points in time increase readers' familiarity with the two, and a slumped Bobby at his bedridden grandfather's door gives particular credibility to the boy's unease and unhappiness with Bob's deterioration. Because of its thoughtful por-

trayal of age, the book has also been used in nursing and retirement homes.

From the opening lines readers will sense the affection between the two characters: "Bobby was named after his best friend, his grandfather, Bob. When Bobby was just a baby, his grandfather told everyone, 'Bobby will be three years old before he can say Grandpa, so I'm going to have him call me Bob.' And 'Bob' was the first word Bobby said." An interesting corollary is found in *Tom*, which begins: "'We're named after each other, Tommy. That's why I want you to call me Tom instead of Grandpa.' So Tommy did."

In *Tom*, again Tommy's Irish

Bobby helping Bob in *Now One Foot, Now the Other*.

grandfather appears. He tells great stories, "some about himself when he was a little boy, and some that he made up. (Tommy loved those the best.)" Then one day Tom, the owner of a butcher shop, teases Tommy into planting chicken heads to grow a "chicken bush." The impatient Tommy can't wait for them to grow and digs them up to check their progress—which, Tom tells him, destroys their chance of survival. DePaola, who enjoyed this kind of humorous banter with his own grandfather, eases it into the story and accompanying pictures with aplomb. Another funny incident occurs when Tom shows Tommy how chicken feet tendons can be manipulated so that the feet seemingly move on their own. Intrigued, Tommy takes two chicken feet home, and after scouring them ("They were kind of smelly"), brightening the claws with red nail polish, and practicing to make them open and close, he takes them to school. His trick scares his friend Jeannie, giving Tommy a good laugh, but it also lands him in a heap of trouble.

Tommy frightens Jeannie with moving chicken claws in *Tom*.

In visually re-creating these incidents, dePaola fashions images ripe with humor. He gives Tommy a self-confident air as he "attacks" his friends with moving chicken feet, building tension toward his inevitable downfall. And when the teacher inadvertently becomes a victim and the principal sends Tommy home with a note—"Tommy is not allowed to bring chicken feet to school ever again"—readers will identify with the chastised boy. Only when Tom, with a big wink, tells him, "We'll just have to think of something else to do. Don't you think?" is Tommy mollified. "Having a grandfather who got you into *that* kind of trouble at school," dePaola said with a chuckle, "was, actually, wonderful!"

DePaola's connection to photography is well employed here as he illustrates a snapshot-style picture of Tom and baby Tommy on the title page, and a second one of Tom and Tommy—set at the time of the story—on the back jacket. Presented in sepia tones, these pictures supply an appropriately old-fashioned flavor and inject a subtle time line into the ongoing dePaola story. They also emphasize the constant affection between grandfather and grandson.

In *The Baby Sister* dePaola expands on family memories from his childhood. In this sweet story a young boy's excitement about the upcoming arrival of a new baby ripples through the pages. Tommy, who already has an older brother, asks his mother for a sister with "a red ribbon in her hair." To help get things ready for the baby's arrival, Tommy paints pictures for the baby's room, whispers, "Hi, baby," to his mother's tummy, and repeats his petition in his nightly prayers, asking God, "Send me a baby sister with a red ribbon in her hair." When his mother goes to the hospital, Tommy's visiting outspoken Italian grandmother, Nana Fall-River, stays with him, instead of Tommy's hoped-for Aunt Nell.[2] An unhappy Tommy, missing his mother, refuses to eat and mopes around the house. However, the sight of Mom waving from the hospital window changes his disposition; he goes home and flings himself into Nana's arms with the words "Let's be friends." And indeed, when Tommy's mother and baby sister arrive

Tommy with his new sibling in the closing image of *The Baby Sister*.

home, it is Nana herself who places the warm bundle in Tommy's lap and pulls back the blanket, revealing baby Maureen with a perky red bow in her hair.

The story's pacing is well managed: pictures appear in a variety of sizes, delivering both flow and continuity to the story. The large, teal-colored wing chair that makes a cameo in *Nana Upstairs & Nana Downstairs*, for instance, provides the setting for several important events in the story and offers emotional focus. It's where Tommy imagines that he and Aunt Nell will read stories together; it's where he unhappily huddles while missing his mother; it's what he hides behind at the homecoming (hoping his mother will ask for him—she does); and it's where he finds a comforting place to hold and meet his long-awaited baby sister.

Queried about the line between fact and fiction in this story, dePaola related that all the basic incidents happened: his request for a baby sister with a red ribbon in her hair, the unwelcome appearance of Nana Fall-River, the "Let's be friends" scene, and the depositing of baby Maureen into his arms. He did, however, make some alterations for the sake of the story. For instance, he condensed the time frame (in those days, mothers were kept in the hospital for as long as ten days) and injected the "chicken pox is going around" line as a reason why Tommy couldn't go to the hospital. That explanation would be easier for today's children to understand, he felt, than the "No children allowed" rule of

Tomie and Maureen in 1945.

1930s hospitals. Modifications of this kind are why dePaola calls these books "autobiographical fiction" and why, in part, he uses "Tommy" rather than "Tomie" for their protagonist's name.

In only two of his early autobiographical tales, *Oliver Button Is a Sissy* and *The Art Lesson*, has dePaola put himself prominently at center stage; in the others, a family member shares the spotlight or the protagonist is part of an ensemble. Published

Hurtful taunts distress Oliver, but he dances into the spotlight anyway.

in 1979, *Oliver Button* was formatted and styled in tune with the original versions of *Nana Upstairs & Nana Downstairs* and *Now One Foot, Now the Other*. Then in 2017 Simon & Schuster art director Laurent Linn gave the story a larger format. This allowed for a more dramatic "stage" for the plot to unfold, which is sure to encourage continued storytime readings and dramatic portrayals.

Illustrated in two colors, with backgrounds void of detail, *Oliver Button Is a Sissy* focuses on a young protagonist who would rather draw or tap-dance than play sports. He is taunted by his classmates until his dance performance shows that he really does have talent.

The plot, which pivots on a serious theme, is lightened with humor and made believable with individualized characters. Any child who has ever been teased by

a classmate—for whatever situation—will relate to Oliver's dismay at having his tap shoes flung around the playground. With the increased awareness of bullying happening in schools today, teachers and librarians will find this a vital story to share. And it is not only children who relate to Oliver's plight. Charles Massey, a New York theatrical manager, gave copies of the book to performers in the musical *A Chorus Line* in its beginning years on Broadway![3]

DePaola named his main character Oliver Button because, he says, he liked the way it sounded—but Oliver's problems, he admits, are ones he encountered in his own childhood. "I could spend hours drawing," dePaola explains, "but I hated sports; nobody ever asked me to play on their ball team because I was so bad at it. But, like Oliver, I was a great tap dancer." DePaola's mother's premonition did, in fact, come true—her son learned to dance, and he became famous. (Some years later, dePaola honored his mother with a book of her own: *My Mother Is So Smart!* relates through the title—and, of course, the story—his closeness to her.)

By the time dePaola tackled the story of his confrontation with his first-grade art teacher in *The Art Lesson*, his skills as storyteller and illustrator had grown. Characters are fleshed out in expression and appearance, line work is brisker, colors are stronger, and backgrounds reflect a more defined sense of place. Written in 1989 in the midst of the growing market for picture books for older children, the story appealed to a wide range of readers. And by naming his protagonist Tommy, dePaola returned to the tradition begun in *Nana Upstairs & Nana Downstairs* of using incidents from his early years as a bridge to his storytelling.

Although the cataloging information for *The Art Lesson* lists the book as fiction, the story is grounded thoroughly in dePaola's real life. The dedication, in fact, divulges that he really did have an art teacher named Mrs. Beulah Bowers. Sharp-eyed readers will find even more clues: a picture on the wall of baby Maureen, mention of Nana Fall-River, a small drawing of brother Joe (sister Judie had not yet been born), a scene of Tom and Nana at their meat counter, and an appearance of Tommy's father in his barbershop.

The final spread depicts a grown-up Tommy at his drawing board, a bowl of popcorn at his side, revealing that Tommy and Tomie dePaola are one and the same. On the wall readers will find images of the shepherd Charlie, Strega Nona, and Bill and Pete, as well as dePaola's signature image, the white bird.

The Art Lesson is more than just a vehicle to tell a family story. It is about a young boy whose drawing abilities have delighted his family for years, but who finds his eager anticipation of school (and art classes) dimmed when he encounters the regimentation of his teacher. Once more dePaola's willingness to build a story around a real-life experience gives children the opportunity to reflect on their own school-centered emotions and concerns.

The warmth and merriment created in *The Art Lesson* extends into his series for older readers, 26 Fairmount Avenue. Just as in his picture books, these stories are about growing up, following one's artistic muse, and—most important—keeping one's individuality.

Through his work as a children's picture-book artist and author, dePaola visited hundreds of schools and talked with an even greater number of children after storytelling programs and in autographing lines. "Children told me a lot over the years," dePaola remembered, "and I discovered that the books they responded to most were the ones based on my own life." They clamored for longer stories, chapter books to accompany them into their next grades in school. At first dePaola rejected the idea;

Clues to the real Tomie dePaola abound in this final spread from *The Art Lesson*.

he had always considered himself an artist first and a writer second. However, as time went on, he began taking the children's requests more seriously, and finally some good-natured prodding from his assistant—who had read many of these same requests in the thousands of letters dePaola received—motivated him to conceive *26 Fairmount Avenue*, becoming the first in a series of eight books under that name and leading him into a new phase of his career.

Using his childhood address in Meriden, Connecticut, as an anchor, dePaola began to spin out childhood incidents, cast in an even stronger autobiographical mode than his picture books. By telling these stories in the first person, he was, at last, Tomie, and the plots became more complex. "It was a different writing

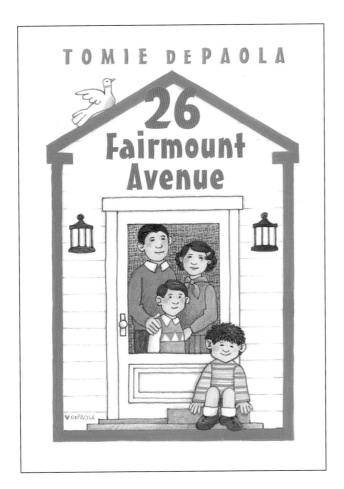

experience," dePaola said. "After years of paring down text to the absolute essentials—necessary in a picture book—I could now use more words to tell my stories and incorporate episodes beyond the picture-book experience."

Reminiscing, dePaola recalled that when the books were still in the planning process, he considered making them strictly textual. But feedback from colleagues, friends, and his publisher convinced him otherwise. Lively black-and-white drawings now pepper the pages, and he has used handwritten diary entries to great effect, adding visual support to the humorous—and sometimes traumatic—events that make up the stories.

The first title begins with the 1938 hurricane that hit the coast of Connecticut when Tomie was four, and follows the family's move to their house in Meriden. DePaola goes on to cover other memorable events from his childhood, such as the commotion he made in the movie theater when the plot of the Disney film *Snow White and the Seven Dwarfs* differed from the story he had heard growing up.

The release of the first book in the spring of 1999 brought positive reviews from critics, librarians, and teachers. Children clamored for more of these funny, poignant stories, and in 2000 the book received a Newbery Honor. In the subsequent books Tomie traces his early childhood years, his disappointments and excitements about going to school, and his continuing childhood antics. In *Here We All Are, On My Way, Things Will Never Be the Same*, and *What a Year*, readers become reacquainted with family members and friends from earlier picture books and are introduced to

26 Fairmount Avenue.

new ones. DePaola sometimes alludes to incidents covered in his picture books as well—being tied into a chair just like Nana Upstairs, for example, or using walls to draw murals while their house was under construction—but he weaves them seamlessly into the larger story, giving the events broader meaning.

As the series continues, World War II breaks out, changing life for everyone and bringing new traumas. While the War Years titles—*I'm Still Scared*, *Why?*, and *For the Duration*—all sensitively cover the early 1940s, contemporary readers may find comfort in stories that resonate with issues and events happening in their world today. In *Why?* the final full-page drawing depicts a young Tomie in pajamas with his back to readers, going off to bed; the scene clearly emphasizes the boy's struggle to understand the "why" of his young world.

26 Fairmount Avenue.

Background materials are often appended to the 26 Fairmount Avenue books for historical context. Pieces on gas rationing, links to popular World War II music, and an excerpt of President Roosevelt's December 8 Pearl Harbor speech provide parents and teachers with even more material for discussion.

While dePaola's work on the acclaimed 26 Fairmount Avenue series took some of his focus away from picture books over the next few years, today he remains best known for his picture-book stories. And one character in particular has endured with a remarkable presence—the beloved grandma witch, Strega Nona.

26 Fairmount Avenue.

an original tale written and illustrated by

Tomie dePaola

Strega Nona

3

Strega Nona

When asked about the provenance of the bulbous-nosed, protruding-chinned character who is so happily familiar to children and adults alike, dePaola told how, while he was doodling on his drawing pad during a faculty meeting many years ago, she just appeared, unannounced and unsolicited.[1] And, he said, she refused to go away!

But dePaola was happy to accommodate her. Through the years, Strega Nona has become a very well-known figure, not only in children's literature but in popular culture as well. And Big Anthony, bumbling though he is—or perhaps because of it—had become a regular presence on the books' stage, sharing adventures with the ever-enduring grandma witch. After Strega Nona revealed "all" in a biography—*Strega Nona, Her Story* (as told to Tomie dePaola)—Big Anthony, not to be left behind, claimed his own top billing in *Big Anthony, His Story*. Soon a third character, the kindhearted Bambolona, joined the pages with Strega Nona and Big Anthony; gradually the threesome began sharing plotlines, with Bambolona staking out her own place in the stories.

Through the years, Strega Nona has earned her creator a Caldecott Honor; has been the star of

Strega Nona and the Twins.

Strega Nona's Magic Ring.

theater dramatizations; has been replicated as a soft cloth doll; has appeared on wall hangings, T-shirts, Christmas ornaments, needlepoint pillows, mugs, and tote bags; was a huge presence during dePaola's presentation at Universal Studios in Orlando, as a gigantic balloon; and has turned up in background details in a number of dePaola's other books. Strega Nona has, indeed, come a long way.[2]

So what makes this grandma witch so enduring? Possibly it's the folkloric quality of the tales, or the combination of silliness and warmhearted truthfulness embedded in the plots, or the child-friendly directness of delivery, or even the Italian aura of sun-warmed colors and brisk lines that enliven the action. More likely it's a blend of these ingredients, and the integrated way in which the artist-author presents them.

Readers first meet Strega Nona in a small village in Calabria, a southern Italian region—and dePaola's ancestral home. There she busily administers potions, cures,

Strega Nona works magic over her pasta pot in *Strega Nona*.

comfort, and advice, carefully portioned with bits of magic—and love. Her pasta pot, for instance, needs three kisses to make it stop boiling—a lesson her bumbling hired helper Big Anthony learns the hard way in *Strega Nona* when he nearly floods the town with pasta (before Strega Nona comes to the rescue).[3] DePaola reveals the secret ingredient of her magic in *Strega Nona, Her Story* when Grandma Concetta passes it on to her young granddaughter (who later becomes a Strega Nona), instructing her, "You must blow three kisses and the pot will stop. For that is the *ingrediente segreto*—LOVE. It is the same with all your magic. Always Love."[4] It has been, of course, dePaola's underlying message to young readers: Love should underscore their work and their lives.

The love ingredient is certainly central to dePaola's work. One sees it in his own interactions with children in library or classroom settings, and in the way he involved them in his books. He treated his characters thoughtfully, infused them with dignity, and injected warmth that radiates off the page. In putting children at the center of what he wrote and illustrated, dePaola created a direct line to their hearts and to their intellects. As Bette Peltola, chair of the 1990 United States Hans Christian Andersen Award committee, wrote in presenting dePaola as the US nominee for the International Board on Books for Young People's illustrator award, "His illustrations capture and reflect the mood of the text and always are clear in meaning to the child reader."[5] Children relate, for example, to how the brusque but kindhearted Strega Nona takes in the awkward Big Anthony, the overworked Bambolona, and the scheming Strega Amelia; and to how she continues to get Big Anthony out of scrapes, sends Bambolona back to her father to help out when times are tight, and wishes her rival, Strega Amelia, the best.

In dePaola's autobiographical stories, the characters of Tommy and others may play out incidents from his childhood, but the heart of the adult dePaola lodges in Strega Nona. While she mixes magic into her spells, dePaola has dispensed magic in another way. In the guise of this toothless, somewhat bossy old woman, he has disseminated messages about being happy with oneself, the need for generosity, and the importance of love. "Children," dePaola said, "are the hope of our future, and we must treat them as such. This may sound trite, but it's true."

Subtle though they are, his messages are ones that children won't miss. Sending a message, however, was never on dePaola's agenda when writing and illustrating: "Books are a fantasy-oriented way to learn basic truths. Truths, not morals. I avoid moralizing at all costs."

Strega Nona herself would be the last person to burden her friends with moral messages; she is far too busy enjoying life—and keeping Big Anthony out of trouble.

In *Strega Nona's Magic Lessons*, Big Anthony continues his bumbling quest to learn Strega Nona's magic spells. Soon, however, his attempts go terribly awry, culminating in a scene in which Strega Nona, he fears, has been turned into a toad—though pictures reveal that she has cleverly bamboozled him again. Does he learn his lesson? Probably not—he is Big Anthony, after all.

"[Strega Nona] didn't have to look twice to know what had happened."—*Strega Nona*

Narrative and image work best when delivered hand in hand, extending each other. This kind of visual synergy—so evident in the Strega Nona stories—is what makes dePaola such a master of the picture-book form. Not only is every page well designed, with careful attention to gutters and margins and the constrictions of the page, but dePaola is highly aware of the flow of the page turns, which are precisely plotted but unobtrusively delivered. The natural limitations of the picture book are built-in considerations for this artist.

From time to time small inconsistencies do creep in—sometimes a bare tree stands beside Strega Nona's house, at other times it's a cypress, and on still other pages it's a stylized design; or a small nearby goat shed appears and disappears without

A tall, gallant Big Anthony in *Strega Nona and the Magic Ring*, LEFT, and RIGHT, Bambolona scolds Big Anthony, and a sly Strega Nona peeks out from the wall in *Strega Nona's Magic Lessons*.

explanation. "It's part of Strega Nona's magic," dePaola claimed with a twinkle in his eye, and who can argue with that?

While children do benefit from the artist's compositional skills, they are more appreciative of the visual extras that appear throughout many of his books. In *Merry Christmas, Strega Nona*, angels peer through Strega Nona's windows, hover over the manger, and smile from rooftops, while singing emanates from red-cloaked shepherds. (Could one be Charlie? The protagonist of *"Charlie Needs a Cloak"* is a frequent background visitor in dePaola's books.) The artist also embeds references from past Strega Nona titles in these books (her hillside house, her animals, her friend Strega Amelia) while allowing each story to stand on its own. In another nod to the visual winks that children enjoy, as well as to dePaola's own playful nature, the newly acclaimed

Strega Nona and Her Tomatoes.

"author" of *Strega Nona, Her Story* poses for her portrait on the back jacket flap, and on the back cover entertains the townspeople at a book signing. And in *Big Anthony, His Story*, dePaola repeats a scene found at the end of Strega Nona's "biography"—the gawky Big Anthony arriving at her door. He repeats the text as well, cleverly joining the two stories together: "The rest is history." And once again dePaola's agile story making causes us to smile.

Because these hijinks, chuckles, and lovable qualities in the first few Strega Nona stories were welcomed by audiences, the artist was prompted to continue dreaming

"The rest is history." While the same text concludes the tales, the illustrations in *Strega Nona, Her Story* and *Big Anthony, His Story* give two different perspectives.

up plots with even more laugh-filled entanglements for Strega Nona to magically unwind. In his 2000 book *Strega Nona Takes a Vacation*, the grandmother witch is off enjoying the sea, and in a good-hearted moment decides to send presents home to her faithful helpers. Slyly, Bambolona keeps the gift of candy for herself and gives Big Anthony the bottle of bubble bath. He heads for the bathtub, and sure enough, disaster strikes. The hilarious scene, reminiscent of the overflowing pasta pot in *Strega Nona*, finds Big Anthony—and the town—awash in bubbles.

The book's title, perhaps, signaled to the author that he himself needed a vacation from the wily grandmother, as it wasn't until 2008 that she made another appearance. In *Brava, Strega Nona! A Heartwarming Pop-Up Book*, she arrived again with great finesse. DePaola worked with pop-up artists Robert Sabuda and Matthew

Reinhart to create amazing visuals as the pages smoothly unfold, offering detailed pop-up scenes with each turn of the page. At the close, Strega Nona champions the special ingredients of food, friends, patience, life, and love.

Other recent titles include *Strega Nona's Harvest*, which finds Big Anthony challenging Strega Nona's gardening proficiencies; *Strega Nona's Gift*, in which Strega Nona and her neighbors prepare treats to celebrate the festivities of the Italian calendar, but Big Anthony's ever-hungry stomach intervenes; and *Strega Nona Does It Again*, which humorously addresses the theme of vanity when Angelina, a beautiful visiting cousin with thoughts for only herself, and handsome young Hugo, who thinks the same way, find that the ever-wise Strega Nona has quietly outmaneuvered them.

Strega Nona Takes a Vacation.

Strega Nona's Harvest.

Over time, sequels can tend to become monotonous to the adult eye (though child readers don't seem to mind) if the author-artist does not tend to the look of the page. DePaola avoids this possibility by varying his page layouts in exciting ways. In *Strega Nona's Harvest*, for example, a full page is balanced with four horizontal bands showing various colorful vegetables. In another spread the vegetables grow in clay pots

Strega Nona's Gift.

alongside the three main characters. As another way of providing a unique look for each book, dePaola varies his color palette to fit the tale. For example, browns and greens are prominent in the gardening story, pinks and blues help identify a seaside setting, and bright holiday colors dominate *Strega Nona's Gift*.

DePaola keeps readers on their toes in other ways too, as with his surprise endings. While the bumbling Big Anthony often gets his comeuppance in the final spread, dePaola sometimes varies this strategy. In *Strega Nona Takes a Vacation*, for example, Strega Nona promises that next time she heads to the sea, she will take her helpers with her—and she includes a happy Big Anthony, with a rubber ducky in his hand. What will they be up to next? DePaola wisely leaves enough space for us to draw our own conclusions—a gift to his readers. He has also been known to include a visual extra to amuse the adult during the reading process. On the back cover of *Strega Nona Takes a Vacation*, for example, in a caricature of Botticelli's *The Birth of Venus*, he depicts a (clothed) Strega Nona rising from the sea on a clamshell, surrounded by birds, flowers, and two flying angels—none other than Bambolona and Big Anthony!

And Strega Nona's reach continues to grow. Early readers will be thrilled to find that the good strega has launched ready-to-read books made just for them. Strega Nona's offer to babysit in *Strega Nona and the Twins*, as well as her hope to harvest and count her ripe tomatoes in *Strega Nona and Her Tomatoes*, lead to some unexpected but delightful turns. And the impressive collection *The Magical World of Strega Nona* not only provides six of the original Strega Nona stories, but also serves up several new and delightful tales to help fill out the Italian grandmother's backstory. Included in the collection are an illustrated map of Strega Nona's *villaggio*, identifying places that have appeared in her stories; a cache of recipes and cooking tips; a "Strega Nona's Little Night Song" lullaby written and read by dePaola (with a CD); and a brief page about dePaola's life. Tucked in between many of the offerings, "Tomie's Notes" offers readers fascinating insights into his pictures and stories. All, of course, illustrated in the artist's distinctive style. A magical world, indeed! But not surprising, when one surveys the magic that dePaola wrapped into and around the many folktales he fashioned through the years.

Strega Nona and the Twins.

Strega Nona and Her Tomatoes.

4

Folktales

olktales, it has been said, are a lifeline to the "humanness" of us all—our foibles, dreams, hurts, and joys. And dePaola's interest in these old stories parallels his interest in people—all kinds of people, all kinds of stories. A longtime reader and researcher of folktales, dePaola did not limit his repertoire to the usual roster of Grimm, Perrault, and Andersen. His penchant ran to folktales rooted in his Italian and Irish heritage and to lesser-known stories from the United States and abroad. Many reflect his humor; some are filled with poignancy; all breathe with the exuberance that the illustrator found throughout his life.

Before beginning the writing or artwork, dePaola did extensive research, looking for the "root tale" and reading every version he could find. Locating sources for *The Legend of Old Befana* found him on the floor of the Library of Congress, surrounded by dozens of titles. As with his other books, ideas for his retellings came sometimes from his family, sometimes from educators he met on speaking and autographing tours, sometimes from collaborators, and sometimes from unexpected places.

Days of the Blackbird, one of the illustrator's strongest offerings, is a case in point. One cold January night some years ago, dePaola ventured out to a nearby restaurant for dinner. His grumbles about the below-zero temperature prompted chef Piero Canuto to say that in his hometown in the northern mountains of Italy, the bitter cold days of

The Legend of the Bluebonnet.

The Legend of Old Befana.

55

January are called *le giornate della merla* ("the days of the blackbird").[1] In Canuto's story once-white doves turned soot black—a color they have remained to this day—when wintry weather forced them to hide in chimney tops to stay warm. Intrigued by this fragment of a legend, dePaola began a research trail that resulted in *Days of the Blackbird*, a book compelling for its narrative and visual authenticity. The artist said that while he considered a lighter approach, he ultimately decided to tip the

Just as her father had promised, the snows would melt, the trees would sprout buds, and then one day, the clear song of La Colomba would fly through the windows and into the Great Hall. She was always the first to return. In no time at all, the courtyard was filled with flowers and birds. Duca Gennaro and Gemma would take their places under the trees and listen to the beautiful melodies.

In *Days of the Blackbird*, La Colomba guides the eye across the double-page spread.

story toward an "Emperor's Nightingale" type of tale. This wise choice allowed him to draw on his love of Italian frescoes and to use a painterly style for his illustrations, which lend a quiet elegance to the book.

In a salute to his key source, dePaola roots the story in Sabbia, Chef Canuto's childhood home. A large full-color photograph of the scene, which hung in Canuto's restaurant, provided inspiration and graphic authority. A double-page-spread title page depicts mountains soaring above the village, and as the book progresses, occasional glimpses of their peaks appear through the high windows and arched doorways of Duca Gennaro's opulent home, the story's main setting. Each afternoon Gemma (which means "jewel" in Italian) and her father, Duca Gennaro (*gennaio* is the Italian word for "January"), enjoy the sweet songs of the many birds that live in their tree-filled courtyard. One bird, a pure white dove that Gemma calls La Colomba, has the clearest melody of all.

When it gets colder and Gemma's father becomes ill, she begs the birds not to fly south, but one by one they leave. Only La Colomba stays, after Gemma convinces her that her singing is what is keeping the duke alive. But during the last frozen days of January, the cold becomes so intense that La Colomba takes to sleeping in a nearby chimney top. When she emerges in the spring, the soot has turned her into *la merla*, the blackbird, which she is still called today. And so, by enlarging the fragment of a story into a full narrative thread and peopling it with intriguing characters and events, dePaola imagines how that old legend might have begun.

Important to the child reader, and hence to dePaola, is what *happens* in a story; action is what charges most of his tales. As in any good literary piece, action must be linked to a strong, believable character who carries the events forward: someone to root for during the climax and cheer for at the conclusion. This necessary element is not lost on dePaola the author or on dePaola the artist. A study of his retellings shows that stringent word choice and fine wielding of the paintbrush can fashion the roots of a tale into highly dynamic portrayals. This is clearly seen in *Days of the Blackbird*, where his depiction of Gemma as an intrepid and determined protagonist is reflected in both text and image.

Another legendary character whom dePaola has brought vividly to life is She-Who-Is-Alone. DePaola first learned about her through Texas reading consultant Margaret Looper, who supplied him with the basics of the tale featured in his book *The Legend of the Bluebonnet*, and who continued to be helpful through the writing and illustrating processes.[2] In this poignant story a young Native American girl bravely sacrifices her beloved doll to the flames to save her people.

As the tale begins, the people call to the Great Spirits to heal their sun-parched land. She-Who-Is-Alone, who has already lost her parents and grandparents to the famine, listens nearby, clasping her beloved warrior doll. When the shaman brings word that rain will come only with the sacrifice of a "most valued possession," She-Who-Is-Alone vows silently to give up her doll. At night she climbs alone to a hilltop, where she flings this most prized possession into the fire. As she does so, her soulful

Drama and emotion emerge through body posture in this scene from *The Legend of the Bluebonnet*.

eyes, the brave tilt of her chin, and the determined hunch to her shoulders form a compelling visual image. For added dramatic impact, dePaola isolates her on the page.

In keeping with the Texas setting, the artist gives this Comanche tale an open, free-flowing appearance. At the beginning he crowds together characters with rounded backs and bowed heads against a stark landscape at the bottom of the page, further expanding the mood with earth-toned clothing and solemn expressions. Then, as She-Who-Is-Alone undertakes her solitary mission, the night sky fills with stars, the red-and-gold flame spirals into a cobalt-blue sky, and the winds scatter the ashes across the heavens. After the morning rain the hills where the ashes fell are covered with blue flowers—a sign of forgiveness from the Great Spirits. Now called bluebonnet, this Texas state flower blankets the countryside each spring. In the scene, dePaola brings white space into play, using it to elicit a feeling of distance; he also introduces a rich palette of greens, yellows, and blues, which balances the presentation and brings deft closure to the tale.

Not all dePaola's choices for folktale retellings are of a serious nature. For instance, the Irish hero Fin M'Coul has rarely been realized with more sidesplitting humor than he is in *Fin M'Coul: The Giant of Knockmany Hill*. Funny indeed is the scene where, in an attempt to fool the nasty Cucullin, Fin rocks away in a cradle, dressed as a baby. But there is more to dePaola's humor than just costuming. Strategic use of space and size is at the center of this comedy.

By placing the text at the bottoms of the pages in this oversize book, dePaola has just the top two thirds left for illustration—a clever device for this particular story. An unadorned brown border edged in pink further restricts the pictorial space so that Fin; his wife, Oonagh; and Cucullin appear as the ample giants they are. To accentuate their size the artist crops their heads at the crown—or, in the case of the mean Cucullin, just above his close-set beady eyes—and at times extends his pictures to the border. This kind of deliberate crowding not only enhances the appearance of size but also punctuates the story's inherent buffoon-

Fin comically cramped into a cradle in
Fin M'Coul: The Giant of Knockmany Hill.

ery. In further playful positioning, small leprechauns and fairies dance at the giant's feet (underneath the cradle) and scuttle around the edges of the pages.

Considering dePaola's impish nature, it seems natural to find such tiny fantastical characters tucked into many of his books. Their presence often adds to the appeal and gives an artistic symmetry to the story. Although they're decorative in *Fin M'Coul,* these creatures can play a dominant role. The pukwudgies (Native American) in Jean Fritz's *The Good Giants and the Bad Pukwudgies* and the tengu (Japanese) in Tony Johnston's *The Badger and the Magic Fan,* both illustrated by dePaola, are mischief-makers of the first degree. A leprechaun (Irish) sets the events in motion in *Jamie O'Rourke and the Big Potato,* trolls (Norwegian) are the ones outwitted in *The Cat on the Dovrefell,* and in *Helga's Dowry* the troll Helga determines the action.

Sure enough, when the sun had set and the night came on, the trolls came down from the hills. What a bunch of creatures—some with tails, some with long, long noses—all of them making a great noise!

The Cat on the Dovrefell.

Rabbit climbing a ladder to the moon in
The Tale of Rabbit and Coyote.

DePaola's own delight in mischief blooms fully in his illustrations for Tony Johnston's *The Tale of Rabbit and Coyote*, a *pourquoi* story about why coyotes howl at the moon. Detractors of dePaola's work who remark on the similarity of his illustrations should look carefully here. Continuing in his folkloric style, the illustrator gives this Oaxacan tale a Mexican flavor. Colors blaze with spicy, sun-hot tones, and stylized shapes echo the designs of primitive folk objects.

The illustrator's facile manipulation of shapes surfaces in several whimsical and distinctive ways. On intensely colored pages, border-decorated squares provide the stage; undulating hills, stylized cacti, and spare-leaved trees fill the background. Coyote and Rabbit, who race across the pages in silly attempts to outdo each other, are smoothly contoured in bright teal and purple. Spanish words, worked into the pictures, often imitate the forms of other objects on the page. All of these elements fuse together, emphasizing the plot's nonsense while anchoring the tale to its place of origin.

Despite finding inspiration in the realm of folklore, however, dePaola is never too concerned about "categories" when a story is in progress; he prefers to think more about how character and action might capture readers. In *Jack* he focuses on a plucky young hero in search of a new life—a take on the everyman sort of character who features in classic "Jack tales." DePaola stretches his ample imagination onto a large canvas and uses every inch to showcase Jack's journey. After Jack declares that he wants to see the world, make new friends, and live in the city, he asks for advice from his grandpa. The old man suggests that the wise and generous king would surely be of help. With his backpack slung over his shoulder, the red-haired boy begins his journey. Before long a yellow chick, a white duck, a pig, a cow, and other animals make up a noisy menagerie of characters that join him on his way to the city.

To cleverly integrate the illustrations into the story, dePaola supplies a rolling path that flows from page to page, mimicking a moveable stage. The sounds of the animals spill out in large colored letters, each one echoing the hues of its owner (green letters for the frog, yellow for the chick, etc.). This allows children to become the animals and join the story, resulting in a noisy but happily participating audience!

"We're going to the city to ask the king for a house," answered Jack.

"Can we come too?"

"Yes, please do."

Jack.

Sharp-eyed children will discover another fascinating addition: dePaola has planted small vignettes of Jack and Jill, Little Red Riding Hood, Jack Be Nimble, Charlie (from *"Charlie Needs a Cloak"*), and an itsy-bitsy spider in the background. At journey's end Jack's friends are merrily ensconced in their new world—although the "noise" now crowding the page is deafening! An afterword notes that dePaola used specially made rubber stamps, reproduced from his own hand lettering, to create the animal "sounds."

Like *Jack, Tomie dePaola's Front Porch Tales & North Country Whoppers* is not quite a folktale, but it also reveals the combined power of story and art, and lets us think about the broader meaning of folklore and its place in our lives. In this fifty-one-page picture book, dePaola has mixed together a variety of original tales, New

Tomie dePaola's Front Porch Tales & North Country Whoppers.

England–style jokes, old yarns, and folk stories, and wrapped them up in colorful pictures that beg laughs on every page. In grouping the stories around the seasons, dePaola adds a sense of continuity and heightens the fun. The back jacket offers a photo of dePaola clad in overalls, greeting "Aiyah" in a conversation balloon. For non–New Englanders a glossary is helpfully appended.

Finally, *Jamie O'Rourke and the Pooka*, a comic folktale from dePaola's Irish background, is his second book about the lazy Jamie O'Rourke and offers typical dePaola humor, which rolls easily off the page. Jamie's wife, Eileen, is off visiting her family, leaving him with a full cupboard; her only instructions are "to do the washin' up each night and a quick swipe with the broom now and then." However, when his old cronies arrive to keep him company, they happily deplete his kitchen stores and leave a mess behind. When a mysterious Pooka arrives to clean up, Jamie thinks he has it made—until he realizes there are dire consequences to a Pooka visit, making him an unhappy man indeed. Using the lighter side of his palette, dePaola contrasts his round, simple faces with a toothy, yellow-eyed, long-eared Pooka, signaling the underlying mischief. And on the back cover a sky-high table full of dirty dishes awaits the lazy Jamie.

Adding an extra punch at story's end is typical dePaola—and is one last treat that fans eagerly await. However, there is more to dePaola than his love of a good joke and well-planned tricks.

Jamie O'Rourke and the Pooka.

The Clown of God.

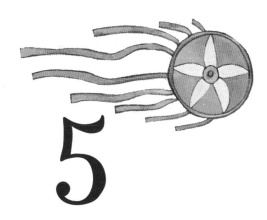

5

Religious and Spiritual Themes

Just as dePaola's folktale-inspired stories emanated from the wellspring of his personal interests and heritage, his religious books arose from his deeply felt spirituality. His early-childhood interest in saints and miracles, as well as his fascination with contemporary liturgical art—which spurred him to enter the Vermont monastery—often surface in the backgrounds of his books. "One of the reasons I became interested in doing books with spiritual themes," the author commented, "was because of the mythic quality of these stories."

His work in this genre reflects his wide interests. There are collections of Bible stories, biographies of saints and other biblical figures, individual tales surrounding holidays, concept-driven board books for toddlers, and retellings of various religious legends. In a response to a question concerning the decisions that go into creating a book on Saint Francis, the Virgin Mary, or the Petook Easter legend, for example, the author conveyed his long-felt desire that "these meaningful stories be available for all children in beautiful formats with well-appointed pictures." And while admitting to a strong interest in the necessary research, he is adamant that the story, above all, must "appeal to the child."

Here, too, lies evidence of dePaola's versatility. For his holiday board books dePaola uses simple, direct, and unadorned pictures, clear shapes, and primary colors, with a focus on the symbols of the occasion.

Patrick hearing God's voice in a dream in *Patrick, Patron Saint of Ireland.*

His biographies (*Patrick, Patron Saint of Ireland* and *Christopher, the Holy Giant*) contain more sophisticated illustrations and more complex narratives, stretching minds and imaginations. These contrasting techniques present a fine example of how the artist conceived his books with attention to the child's mind and eye and concern for the ways children process thoughts.

For example, in retelling the life of Ireland's patron saint, Patrick—which dePaola's Irish mother had prodded him to write and illustrate for many years— dePaola uses forceful lines; varied shades of greens, blues, and golds; and a highly stylized approach. Patrick's life unfolds through isolated events, linked through frieze-like panels that concentrate on one incident per image. By choosing this method, the artist keeps his text simple, injecting the needed emotion into artwork that has been embellished with Celtic symbols. The book closes with five legends, each with its own illustrations. As in the main text, these stories are written without much detail, allowing the artwork to carry the drama. It is a very suitable portrayal for the life of this monastic man.

Christopher, the Holy Giant follows a similar pattern, although because it is based on a single legend rather than on the entire life of a person, the telling is more cohesive. Colors are more vivid, and images, especially those of Christopher, are appropriately larger. Particularly compelling is the scene of Christopher carrying the Christ Child across a stormy river. Derived from a fresco dePaola found on a column in the Basilica of San Petronio in Bologna, Italy, the striking image brings power to the page. As a host of angels sing above, a struggling Christopher perseveres through swirling patterns of blue and green waves—with the Christ Child on his back, beautifully highlighted against a bright full moon.

In *The Lady of Guadalupe*, dePaola recounts a Mexican story about a poor farmer named Juan Diego who is singled out by the Mother of God to carry a message to the bishop, telling him to build a church in her honor. After Juan is twice dismissed, the Lady tells him to return to the bishop and to take the beautiful Castilian roses that have now appeared on the once-barren hilltop. Juan gives the bishop the roses, but what impresses the church father is the image of the Lady now imprinted on Juan's rough-fibered tilma cloak. At last the bishop heeds the request and builds a church on the spot of the Lady's visitation. DePaola celebrates this miracle in an oversize book that is rendered in colors and designs found in Mexican folklore. It was translated into a well-received Spanish edition by Pura Belpré.[1]

The Lady of Guadalupe.

"The further he went, the higher the water rose and the heavier the child became."—*Christopher, the Holy Giant*

Mary, the Mother of Jesus.

The Mother of God in *The Lady of Guadalupe* is rendered as a more mature woman—saddened, perhaps, by the world's woes and griefs that she witnesses from the heavens—than the Mary in *Mary, the Mother of Jesus*. DePaola divides this story into chapters, depicting the incidents of Mary's life from birth to Ascension. Formal illustrations that fill the page are complemented by smaller, more symbolic images that decorate the pages of text. Mary's countenance subtly changes across the book, from shy bride, to wondrous mother, to bereaved viewer at the Crucifixion, to receiver of the Holy Spirit, and finally to Holy Mother. The pastel palette takes on denser hues at times—depending on what is being portrayed—adding richness to the story.

In response to a question about the puzzling image on the jacket, of Mary holding an apple—a fruit usually associated with Eve in the Garden of Eden—dePaola cites a book on church symbolism that states that the apple is "sometimes given to the Virgin Mary, for it was her Son who took away the curse of sin."[2] It was a device that medieval painters often used, dePaola said. He, too, has included such devices in his art. "I am a stylized—not a realistic—painter, and I often use symbolic representations in my work." The artist points to *The Clown of God* for another example of his use of symbolism; in the book's final pages, he shows a partial view of a window where none appeared before. The window, dePaola said, represents the clown's redemption and the release of his soul to the heavens.

The life of Saint Francis of Assisi was one dePaola had wanted to explore for many years, and the celebration of the saint's eight hundredth birth anniversary in 1982 seemed the perfect time.[3] In doing so, dePaola returned (figuratively) to Italy, with its traditional red-tiled roofs and soft-colored stonework. His resulting biography, *Francis, the Poor Man of Assisi*, glows with rich paintings, executed in transparent inks, that appear as full-page images on the right-hand side of each spread. The juxtaposed text on each left-hand page has a large illuminated-style initial letter. And, similar to the format used in *Mary, the Mother of Jesus*, at page bottom small vignettes provide balance as well as additional detail for the larger picture.

In an endeavor to present the humble yet remarkable life of Saint Francis authentically, dePaola made two research trips to Italy (noted in the book's fore- and afterwords), to see where the monk carried out his mission, and to study the frescoes of Francis and his companion, Saint Clare. But close examination of his illustrations reveals that while dePaola obviously did his homework, his poignant visual descriptions result mainly from a greater reach into his own artistic well. Characterizations are deepened through individualized facial expressions, fluid body movements, the tilt of a head, and, particularly, the position of the hands. While dePaola's dots-for-eyes, line-for-mouth technique was appropriate for many of his more lighthearted titles, his insightful rendering here is what the subject demands, and dePaola clearly delivers. Even *The Lady of Guadalupe*, which also contains more fully realized character depictions, doesn't project quite the same pathos and jubilance found in the characters in *Francis*.

On the dust jacket, for example, the angle of the branches and leaves and the placement of the birds on one side, the still figure of the man on the other, force the eye to page center, where Saint Francis's graceful, expressive hands are frozen midgesture. From the joy Francis emanates when he dances as a young beggar ("I am God's fool") to the radiant song that erupts from his pain-racked body on his deathbed, dePaola captures the essence of this remarkably devoted man. DePaola often "borrows" from the masters—this time from Giotto. One need only look at Giotto's *St. Francis Preaching to the Birds* to see an intriguing resemblance in the positioning of the hands.[4]

DePaola returned to Saint Francis in 2009 with *The Song of Francis*, the tale of a lonely young monk who wants only to sing and to tell people of God's great love, but he is all alone. One day the small yellow-haired

Francis, the Poor Man of Assisi.

angel who follows him everywhere whispers to Francis that he must sing, for "God will hear you. And so will I." As the monk begins, birds and angels of every shade and color fill the sky, and at last Francis is happy. When dusk falls and the cherubs leave, Francis promises the small angel that the next day he will sing again. This whole book gleams with color—from splashy, tropical-toned endpapers that feature pink and violet flowers, to all the pages in between, which swirl with multicolored birds, brightly hued plants, and a rush of angels. Angels make frequent appearances in dePaola's books, and they feature prominently in two other charming titles: *Pascual and the Kitchen Angels* and *Angels, Angels Everywhere*. These stories give vent to dePaola's sly humor, as angels in various guises romp across the pages, dispensing good feelings and many laughs through their activities and antics.

DePaola visually celebrates life in two other vibrantly colored books with a spiritual bent. Flowered endpapers once again set the scene for *Let the Whole Earth Sing Praise*, where the illustrations were inspired, dePaola said, by the folk art of the Otomi people of Puebla, Mexico. The hand-lettered text, which derives from two pieces of Old Testament Scripture, praises all things on the earth and in the sky—a tribute to our planet. Similar in tone and message, *Look and Be Grateful* urges children to open their eyes each morning to the world around them—and to be thankful for it. A particularly delightful page depicts differently colored hands reaching out among flowers seemingly afloat, accompanied by just two words: "BE GRATEFUL."

Let the Whole Earth Sing Praise.

Alongside flowers, angels, white birds, and hearts—which have become common features in dePaola's books—the moon also has a special place. It often appears in its various phases in his artwork, and can lend his books a spiritual feel. One such compelling tale, conceived by revered storyteller Patricia MacLachlan and illustrated by dePaola, is *The Moon's Almost Here*. Some forty years ago, in the early stages of their careers, the two created *Moon, Stars, Frogs, and Friends*; this more recent work displays how each has grown in his or her approach to story and to art. In the illustrations dePaola cleverly plays off his earlier book *Sing, Pierrot, Sing*. That story featured the heartsick mime Pierrot, who is able to overcome the loss of his sweetheart, Columbine, when the children urge him to dance and sing with them under the moon. In *The Moon's Almost Here*, dePaola returns to Pierrot, showing him and his son as they await the arrival of the full moon with great anticipation. Each turn of the page builds excitement as the two watch a kitten, a chick, a butterfly, and a puppy settle in for the night, until finally moonrise comes, "so big and so bright." The white-clothed characters, an ideal contrast to the soft shades of twilight,

The Moon's Almost Here.

"The moon's almost here,"
Clucks plump mother hen.
Chicks settle under her,
Safe in their pen.

The moon's almost here.
The butterfly knows.
She sits on a flower,

Then—
Quickly she goes.

He curls in a ball
And closes his eyes.

Good night little dog.
Dreams in your head.

Good night little kitten,
Warm in my bed.

And so bright.

The Moon's Almost Here.

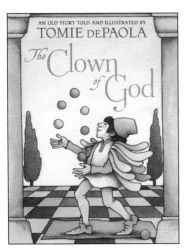

DePaola's cover for *The Clown of God* has its visual origins in a
preliminary jacket for *Our Lady's Juggler*, a book never completed.

bring a quiet simplicity to the pages, matched by MacLachlan's eloquent wording. It is a memorable contribution from both author and artist.

Moving from the world of Pierrot to that of a different clown, we come to one of the most profound and splendidly illustrated stories of dePaola's career: *The Clown of God*. The beginnings of this book are lodged in an old French tale, "Our Lady's Juggler," which dePaola remembered from his childhood. His research eventually took him to a story by Anatole France, and from there to a much earlier medieval source that had a "Mary's tale" (about the mother of Jesus) as its basis. DePaola reshaped the story, adding a Christmas component, and flavored it—especially through the illustrations—with Italian backgrounds and costumes.

Placing his story in Sorrento at the beginning of the Renaissance, dePaola portrays an orphaned beggar boy named Giovanni, who happily entertains the market crowds with his juggling talents. When a passing theatrical troupe agrees to take Giovanni under its wing, the boy eagerly goes with them. He puts on a clown face and attracts increasingly bigger crowds in each town with his tricks, until, a master of his art, he takes off on his own. Traveling the length and breadth of Italy, he mesmerizes the people by juggling sticks, plates, rings, and burning torches—always finishing with the "Sun in the Heavens," where balls of many colors, topped by a golden orb, flash and tumble, rainbowlike, in the sky.

One day Giovanni meets two monks on the road who tell him that his talent is a gift from God, and that the founder of their order, Brother Francis (referring to Saint Francis of Assisi), said, "If you give happiness to people, you give glory to God as well." Years pass, and Giovanni continues to entertain, but as he ages, his hands become less nimble and his feats passé.

One day, between two towns, Giovanni was sitting in the shade of a tree, eating a lunch of bread and cheese. Two Little Brothers came down the road.

"Will you share your food with us, good clown," they asked, "for the love of God and the blessings of our Brother Francis?"

"Sit down, good fellows," Giovanni said. "There is more than enough."

As the three men ate, the two Little Brothers told Giovanni how they went from town to town, begging their food and spreading the joy of God.

"Our founder, Brother Francis, says that everything sings of the glory of God. Why, even your juggling," said one of the brothers.

"That's well and good for men like you, but I only juggle to make people laugh and applaud," Giovanni said.

"It's the same thing," the brothers said. "If you give happiness to people, you give glory to God as well."

"If you say so!" said Giovanni, laughing. "But now I must be off to the next town. *Arrivederci*, good brothers—and good luck!"

The Clown of God.

Finally, when his aging fingers cause him to drop the rainbow of balls, and people laugh, Giovanni vows to give up his juggling. He becomes a beggar once again and slowly heads back home to Sorrento. Arriving on a cold, dark night, he takes refuge in the monastery church of the Little Brothers of Saint Francis and falls asleep. He awakens to ethereal music, blazing candlelight, and a procession of people laying gifts at the feet of the ancient and revered statue of the Lady and the Child. It is Christmas Eve.

Later, after everyone has gone, Giovanni creeps close to the statue. Although he has no gift to leave for the Christ Child, he is moved by the solemn expression on the Child's face. Remembering that he "used to make people smile," Giovanni puts on his clown face once more, and he begins to juggle. Up fly his rings and sticks, plates and balls; never has he performed the "Sun in the Heavens" so well. But suddenly his poor heart gives out, and Giovanni falls to the floor. When the brothers arrive, they find the old man dead—but the golden ball lies securely in the Christ Child's hand, and a smile touches the Child's face.

The tale offers intellectual stimulation and emotional engagement, while providing a message about valuing one's own talents; and dePaola's illustrations are complex, with their strategic use of page composition, color, texture, character portrayal, and pace. The illustrations also show, as do many of dePaola's books, the decided influence of such early Renaissance painters as Fra Angelico, Giotto, Botticelli, and Piero della Francesca. Subtly fashioned details add dimension and provide backbone to the story's inherent dramatic power.

The title page nicely sets the scene. Villagers gather around a festooned open-air stage on which a masked clown holds high a tambourine. On the stage's backdrop a rainbow of ribbons announces the book's title and author. In the beginning pages, pastel colors shaded with earthy tones give texture and are balanced with white space, creating a lighthearted, open look. Later, as things start to go poorly for Giovanni, the white space disappears. Darkly clouded skies, deep-toned hills and trees, and gray cathedral walls signal a change of mood and the coming of the story's climax. They also adroitly serve as an emotional counterpoint to the colorful final image, when readers see the golden ball in the hands of the smiling Christ Child.

As the story develops, the focus placed on the protagonist changes. At the start, Giovanni appears quite small and is, at times, just a figure in the crowd. Later, as his talents grow, he takes a more prominent place on the page. When he first performs the "Sun in the Heavens" trick, he appears center stage, the crowd relegated to the periphery. And when the story ends and Giovanni falls at the foot of the statue, arm reaching out, dePaola places him low on the page, his juggling accoutrements spilled around him, the walls of the cathedral arching above—a fine composition that delivers the dramatic impact the scene demands.

But Giovanni didn't hear or notice him.
"And now," said Giovanni, smiling at the face of the Child,
"First the red ball, then the orange...."

Young Giovanni's juggling is echoed in the elderly Giovanni's last performance before the statue of the Christ Child in *The Clown of God*.

Architectural, geographical, and costume details help anchor the story in time and place. For example, dePaola presents varied scenes as "Up and down Italy [Giovanni] traveled." In one scene, country peasants with hoes and bales of straw watch the juggler perform; in another, Venetian gondoliers ply their boats. DePaola, who has long given thought to diversity, included a black gondolier after finding a similar image in Carpaccio's *The Miracle of the Relic of the True Cross on the Rialto Bridge.*[5] Again, borrowing (but not copying) from the great masters is something dePaola does freely; it not only adds richness to the illustrations, but also gives adults excellent opportunities to lead children from the picture books they know to the great art that they might one day see in museums around the world.

The Clown of God.

77

Guess Who's Coming to Santa's for Dinner?

6

Christmas Stories

DePaola happily acknowledged that Christmas, his favorite holiday, had been important to him since his childhood, when his home was filled with "lots and lots of lights, many good things to eat, and crowds of friends and relatives." Through the years a decrease in time and energy toned down his celebrations, but that didn't mean his love affair with the holiday had lessened. Instead it wound its way into a variety of books about Christmas, in funny tales (*Santa's Crash-Bang Christmas*); illustrated versions of carols (*The Friendly Beasts*); collections (*Tomie dePaola's Book of Christmas Carols* and *Christmas Remembered*); various retellings of Christmas stories (*The Christmas Pageant*, *The Legend of Old Befana*, and *The First Christmas: A Festive Pop-Up Book*); and poignant stories that often leave a profound message beyond their Christmas theme (*Pages of Music* and *Country Angel Christmas*).

When Simon & Schuster began to reissue a number of dePaola's out-of-print books in 2015, one that they selected was a particular favorite of the artist-author's: *The Legend of Old Befana: An Italian Christmas Story*. The book, based on a tale about how Old Befana visits all children on the Feast of Three Kings (January 6), follows her search for the Christ Child. And while she never reaches Bethlehem, her quest and its consequences have become part of Italian Christmas lore. A larger format, a fresh design, and a deepening of colors

The Legend of Old Befana: An Italian Christmas Story.

have given new life to and added to the warmth and humanity of this 1980 classic—now available to a new generation of children.

In *The Christmas Pageant*, dePaola's love of the holiday merges with his love of theater. To tell the familiar biblical story, he chose simple, straightforward words to match young children's understanding, and supplied a stage setting for the unfolding plot. Children in costumes (donned on the title page), sheep on wheels, and angels and stars hanging from rafters play out the Christmas Eve story in a very childlike and effective way.

Tomie dePaola's Book of Christmas Carols, on the other hand, represents the more regal side of the artist's oeuvre. It includes luminescent colors resembling stained glass; stylized folk objects; a formal balance of text, art, and white space; and three gatefolds that not only bring a linear pageantry to those pages, but also carry a sense of elegance through the whole book.

Two other Christmas books, *The Night Before Christmas* and *An Early American*

SHE WAS RUNNING IN THE SKY!

. . . It was a night of miracles.

The Legend of Old Befana: An Italian Christmas Story.

A nativity wreath with characters based on Tomie's artwork adorns his front door.

Christmas, deserve special scrutiny not only for their artistic merit, but also for the connections dePaola makes that enrich each of these works. DePaola set his version of Clement Moore's well-known poem in the 1840s, an appropriate and fascinating choice considering the poem's history.[1] Moore, a professor of Greek and Hebrew at New York's General Theological Seminary, wrote the poem as a Christmas gift to his children in 1822. Although Moore first published it (anonymously) in 1823 in the *Troy Sentinel*, a New York newspaper, he did not acknowledge himself as the author until 1837. And it wasn't until 1844 that he included "A Visit from St. Nicholas" (the poem's actual title) in one of his own anthologies, coinciding with its wide acceptance as a beloved Christmas tradition. In choosing the 1840s for his setting, dePaola parallels the time when readers were becoming universally aware of the poem's existence.

Guess Who's Coming to Santa's for Dinner?

Inspiration for the title-page illustration in *The Night Before Christmas*, RIGHT, derived from his then home, a nineteenth-century farmhouse in Wilmot Flat, New Hampshire, ABOVE.

While researching the ballad, dePaola discovered that Moore had undoubtedly been influenced by Washington Irving's *Diedrich Knickerbocker's History of New York from the Beginning of the World to the End of the Dutch Dynasty*, in which the famous American story-teller makes reference to Saint Nick. Not only did Moore follow Irving's penchant to depict Saint Nick as a sturdy, pipe-smoking Dutchman, but Moore's use of phrases such as "chubby and plump" and "laying his finger aside of his nose" was also probably influenced by Irving's text. Some 158 years later, dePaola followed Moore's lead, illustrating a pudgy, twinkly-eyed Saint Nicholas who is a "right jolly old elf," and fashioning diminutive figures to suggest "a miniature sleigh with eight tiny reindeer."

Using the small New Hampshire town of Wilmot Flat (where dePaola lived at the time) as a background—and his own house in particular—the artist imbues the book with a rural New England flavor that sets this version apart from the many "anywhere" renditions available. He extends the ambience by wrapping his presentation in quilt designs, many of which are from his own New England quilt collection. This motif is carried out prudently. Multicolored square and diamond quilt-patterned borders frame the front of the jacket, and the family members sleep "snug in their beds" under cheerily colored quilts within the story. While line rather than color is generally thought to be the means of energizing a story, here it is the dense hues that set each spread aglow and encourage the all-important turn of the page. Of executing the illustrations, dePaola revealed that he chose colored inks on coarse paper so that the transparencies, used in the printing process at that time, would pick up the texture.

The outdoor scenes depict a Wilmot Flat that hasn't changed much in the last hundred or so years, complete with a war memorial statue, the local Baptist church, and clapboard houses. The interior scenes are authentic to the time period: a plaid-covered wing chair stands near the fireplace, flowery stencils embellish a wall, woven rugs brighten wooden floors, and candles and kerosene lamps look ready for use. And, ever cognizant of the child reader, the artist punctuates the pages with early-nineteenth-century toys—wooden soldiers, striped balls, spinning tops, pull toys, hobbyhorses, soft dolls, and candy canes. When the book was published, dePaola held a celebration for Wilmot Flat residents in the town hall—a sign of his generosity and delight in Christmas festivities.

An Early American Christmas is another of dePaola's holiday-themed books that is set, though somewhat earlier, in 1800s New Hampshire. It features a blond-haired, angular father whose physical proportions could identify him as an ancestor of the father in dePaola's *The Night Before Christmas*. Having moved from Wilmot Flat to nearby New London by the time *An Early American Christmas* was published, dePaola chose a more generic setting for this historical-fiction picture book.

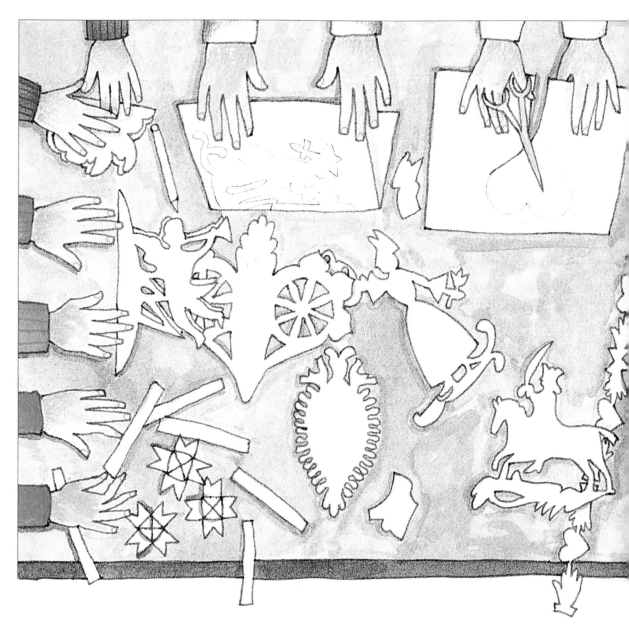

In the story a family of German immigrants have brought their many Christmas traditions with them to New England. Throughout the busy year they ready their home for the holiday: dipping candles, storing the best apples, whittling a new character for the manger scene, creating paper tree decorations, baking cookies, and choosing a tree in the forest. On Christmas Eve, as a candle shines from each window in the house and the sound of carols drifts over the countryside, their neighbors come to see and listen. Next year they, too, will enfold these beautiful traditions into their lives—traditions that will, of course, become part of the holiday across America and around the world.

In presenting his part-historical, part-fictional tale, dePaola expands on his signature folkloric style, creating some mesmerizing spreads. Immediately noticeable is

An artistic array of hands conveys the family's busy preparations for the Christmas holiday in *An Early American Christmas*.

the vast amount of white space. Spare, well-composed, and nicely spaced artwork is thoughtfully balanced by decorative details (a stylized evergreen, floating stars and hearts, geometric designs, and an almost ever-present cat). His soft-hued palette, shaded for texture, aptly reflects the colors of Christmas, and by also incorporating a lot of white within the pictures, the artist injects the wintry atmosphere he wants. This technique results in a far different kind of winter setting from the one found in *The Night Before Christmas*, which—except for the snow scenes—is rich with color. Although close in subject matter and time period, these two books are rendered in different, yet equally appropriate, ways.

Written in 1987, *An Early American Christmas* reflects an interest in immigration

One of Tomie's Christmas trees featuring ornaments based on his art.

and traditions passed down through families that was present at the time of publication. On the penultimate page the text reads, "As the years went by, some of the neighbors put candles in their windows too. Then Christmas trees appeared in their parlors. They began to sing Christmas songs. One by one every household in the village became a Christmas family."

More recent Christmas books continue to differ dramatically in story and artistic approach but nevertheless remain true to the author's love of storytelling. As previously discussed, *Strega Nona's Gift* cleverly showcases Italian Christmas customs while imbuing the old woman with her usual craftiness and kindness. And in *Guess Who's Coming to Santa's for Dinner?* (it is *not* Strega Nona!), dePaola takes readers on an increasingly hilarious spin as Christmas nears. A busy Mrs. Claus welcomes more and more family to the North Pole, houseguests become ever-more boisterous, gifts are wildly exchanged, Santa returns from his midnight delivery service, a pageant is performed, and snowballs are volleyed about

Guess Who's Coming to Santa's for Dinner?, ABOVE and BELOW.

until—finally—Christmas dinner is served. The continued comings and goings are cheerfully narrated in text boxes or balloons, with the merriment growing in tandem with each turn of the page. Sharp-eyed readers will spy the shenanigans of one particular guest, while *all* will sense the mayhem—as well as the fun. Children inspired by this book may well delight in writing personal versions of their own holiday experiences with visiting friends and family.

COME TO THE PAGEANT AT FOUR
NO PETS ALLOWED, ESPECIALLY OSCAR

"Children, come with me! Let's go into the library. We are going to put on a Christmas pageant for the family before dinner."

LISBETH AND LINA, YOU WILL BE ANGELS.

ERIK, YOU WILL BE A SHEPHERD.

LUKAS, YOU WILL BE A SHEEP.

EMIL AND LIEF, YOU WILL BE A CAMEL. EMIL IN THE FRONT. LIEF IN THE BACK.

EMMA, MY LITTLE PET, YOU WILL HOLD MY SPEAR WHILE I SING!

BABY WILLIE, YOU WILL STAY OUT OF THE WAY!

AND I WILL BE THE CHRISTMAS STAR!

The Birds of Bethlehem.

DePaola drew from a completely different artistic well in *The Birds of Bethlehem*, as he imagined the Nativity story told through the eyes of a flock of gathering birds. Painted with opaque acrylics on handmade watercolor paper, the story features glowing colors strengthened by strong lines that heighten the awe of the coming event. The chattering birds, in an array of shades from yellow and red to deep green and blue, watch as a long line of people—including a man and a robed woman riding a donkey—cross a far hill. As the birds relate scenes of the early-morning birth in a nearby inn, they also tell of a golden angel appearing in the sky, and a choir singing from the heavens. The story closes with Mary, Joseph, and the Baby carefully protected in the manger, with the exquisite birds hovering in the eaves. It is an evocative telling matched by beautifully rendered, memorable illustrations.

Christmas Remembered, a collection of autobiographical stories marketed for "all ages," includes a variety of incidents revealed in dePaola's 26 Fairmount Avenue books. In chronological order dePaola recounts memories of Christmases past, starting from when he was three and following him to places such as his childhood home in Meriden, Connecticut; Brooklyn, while at Pratt Institute; Weston Priory in Vermont, during his time as a novice; San Francisco, where he studied at the California College of Arts and Crafts and worked out of a bayside apartment; and Whitebird, his present home in New Hampshire.

Amusing, insightful, and full of spirit, the remembrances are accompanied by luscious illustrations that add an extra zest to the telling. Whether it's a full-page image of tissue-paper roses used yearly on his Christmas tree; a rendition of a handmade, heart-shaped pin he once gave his mother; or an outdoor snow scene of a white bird (with a heart) sitting on a fence beneath a shining star, each illustration adds evidence of his love and deep feelings for the Christmas season.

Writing Is Like Cooking

by Tomie dePaola

I like to cook at Christmas—or at any time, for that matter—and I believe that writing a good manuscript is like making a good stock. You start by throwing all your scraps (your ideas)—onion peel, potato peel, carrot peel, old bones, you name it—into a pan of water. As that heats up, scum begins rising to the surface. It is very important to scoop that scum off the top of the liquid and get rid of the impurities from all the stuff you've put in. As the scum rises, you need to continue to skim it off, and that takes a long time. One must be very patient. After all the scum is gone, you bring the stock to a soft rolling boil so there is a little more activity. The longer you let that stock (the experiences) slowly simmer, the more the essential flavors can come out of the ingredients. Now, at this point, you taste the stock and boost the flavor by adding some peppercorns, some salt, some spices, letting them simmer together. Then, with layers of cheesecloth, you strain the stock, throwing all the leftovers away.

The next step is to take the liquid and reduce it to make the flavors strong. You may begin with three gallons and end up with only a half gallon—the more you reduce, the stronger the flavors will be. But your stock still is not finished. You have to continue to be patient and let it slowly boil away. If you want that stock (your plot) to be crystal clear, then you beat an egg white and its shell into the cold stock, which means you have to take it off the stove and let it sit for a while.

Now you heat the stock up again very slowly, removing the last of the impurities that the egg white has brought to the surface. Then, very carefully, dip a ladle into the stock, remove it spoonful by spoonful, and hold it up to the light. Now you have a beautiful, crystal clear, full-flavored stock. And that is just the way writing works.

When creating a picture book, you need to get down to the basic essentials. Of course, this varies somewhat depending on the book. A board book is like a snack—there are just a few words and only six illustrations, but an elaborate book, such as *The Legend of the Poinsettia*, is like a banquet with its many courses.

"Old Mother Goose / When she wanted to wander / Would ride through the air / On a very fine gander."
—*Tomie dePaola's Mother Goose*

7

Mother Goose and Other Collections

Strong storytelling is evident in *Tomie dePaola's Mother Goose* from the very beginning. The front matter, for example, features several images of a young boy and girl reading on a pillowed bench. Readers see the duo as bookends; above them is a picture of a goose. The half-title page rearranges these images: the girl is now reading aloud to the boy, who is holding a stuffed white goose in his hands; the goose picture has been replaced by a window looking out onto billowing clouds. To complete the connection, the book's final illustration finds the two children fast asleep, the book spread open on the girl's lap, while in the sky above, a silhouetted Mother Goose sails off across a full moon. Playwright Connie Congdon cleverly used these children as lead-ins to the story when writing a stage adaptation of the book for the Minneapolis Children's Theatre Company.[1]

The connection between child appeal and artistry continues on the title page, where a smiling, bonneted woman is seen beckoning to a large white bird. Then we find, juxtaposed with the first page of text, Mother Goose in flight on the goose's back, waving. She seems to be saying, *Come along. This reading adventure is about to begin.*

The creation of this 128-page collection happened in a roundabout way when then editor, Margaret Frith, arrived in New London for a work session one spring in the early 1980s. Frith noted the five Mother Goose paintings pinned to the wall of dePaola's studio—which the artist had just completed for the upcoming Illustrators' Exhibition at the Children's Book Fair in Bologna, Italy.[2] Struck by the imaginative spirit of the renderings, she suggested that dePaola think about creating a Mother Goose book of his own, to which dePaola replied, "Oh, sure, Margaret, the world really needs another Mother Goose!" But several weeks later the idea was revitalized when dePaola's London editor, Joy Backhouse, saw the five illustrations in Bologna.[3] She suggested turning the artwork into accordion-folded story streamers depicting four Mother Goose verses, and publishing them as a joint venture between Methuen (her company) and Putnam. *Tomie dePaola's Mother Goose Story Streamers* was released in 1984 on both sides of the Atlantic. *Tomie dePaola's Mother Goose* made its appearance the following year.

An array of brushes in dePaola's studio.

But with hundreds of Mother Goose books available—new ones constantly coming onto the market, and others that remain fresh in people's memories—the question arose: How does one go about turning an old theme into a unique new rendition? "The design factor" is how dePaola characterized it when explaining the process that he, Frith, and the Putnam art director at the time, Nanette Stevenson, worked through to bring to completion the large-format, full-color collection that became *Tomie dePaola's Mother Goose*.[4]

Tomie dePaola's Mother Goose.

In doing his research, dePaola read every version of every verse he could find. But when making his selections, he used, wherever possible, the classic verses collected by English folklorists Peter and Iona Opie. He also took to heart their advice in *The Oxford Nursery Rhyme Book*, which suggests that any Mother Goose for young children needs to have not only each rhyme illustrated but also every stanza of the longer rhymes as well.[5] With this in mind, dePaola and Frith worked closely, winnowing the choices carefully to allow for the "open and light" format that dePaola wanted. Their goal was to include a mix of well-known verses with less familiar fare. For his illustrations, dePaola "used a dark brown line to delineate the stylized figures and settings, concentrating on simple shapes and clarity of composition."

In the meantime, Stevenson constructed a grid, mapping out the book page by page to ensure a natural flow and harmony. As a result, images appear on double-page spreads, single pages, or half pages; as vertical borders; or as individual spots that sometimes surround, sometimes adjoin, but always give both variety and unity to the book.

Once the grid was established and the selections were firm, design decisions were made about type, size, margins, and more. Then dePaola began to work on

Baa, baa, black sheep,
 Have you any wool?
Yes, sir, yes, sir,
 Three bags full;
One for the master,
 And one for the dame,
And one for the little boy
 Who lives down the lane.

The cock's on the roof top
 Blowing his horn,
The bull's in the barn
 A-threshing the corn,
The maids in the meadow
 Are making the hay,
The ducks in the river
 Are swimming away.

Tomie dePaola's Favorite Nursery Tales.

the more than three hundred full-color illustrations. Which image did he start with? "I wanted," dePaola explained, "to establish the image of Mother Goose on the dust jacket, which the marketing department needed for catalog copy and to start work on the publicity. It was important to me that even though you don't see Mama Goose (my nickname for the spry lady) throughout the book, her presence be identified. We (Margaret and I) discussed at length whether she should be seen in profile (my preference) or in full face (Margaret's choice); you can see who won! I did get my way on the title page, where you see Mother Goose complete with finger pointing outward, an image I remembered from an early version in my childhood."[6]

The *Mother Goose* team's time and efforts were rewarded. The book is now considered a classic in the Mother Goose genre. And dePaola's interpretation of Mother Goose herself is a winner. She has enough homespun attributes (glasses, gray hair, apron, and buckled shoes) to play the part, while her dapper attire (driving gloves; a debonair hat trimmed with a long, curling feather; and bright red stockings) adds class.

Throughout the pages, dePaola's color choices—clear pinks, violets, blues, goldenrods, and teal greens—glow against pure white space, allowing the comic undertones to flourish. Diversity of character is evident: faces showing a variety of eyes, complexions, and hair styles shine from the pages. And there is diversity in the presentation as well. Some of the rhymes are illustrated in a straightforward manner ("Rub-a-dub-dub" shows three men in a tub), while others exhibit an inventive dimension (in "The cat goes fiddle-i-fee," each visual vignette grows larger as the cumulative verse grows longer; and a single white-sided barn serves as the setting for both "Baa, baa, black sheep" and "The cock's on the rooftop").

In 1986 dePaola reprised his *Mother Goose* success with another collection, *Tomie dePaola's Favorite Nursery Tales*. The wraparound jacket features a boy reading aloud to two other children amid an assortment of teddy bears and dolls, and the artist references his earlier book with a picture of Mother Goose on the back cover.

In *Nursery Tales*, dePaola relied on selections that his mother had shared with him as a child. In fact, the dedication reads, "To my mother, Flossie Downey dePaola, whose lap I sat on a long time ago, and listened to her tell me many of these stories." The choices, which come mostly from familiar sources—Joseph Jacobs, Aesop, the Brothers Grimm, Hans Christian Andersen, and P. C. Asbjørnsen—are told with wit and warmth and are presented with panache.

Tomie dePaola's Favorite Nursery Tales.

DePaola's next ventures as anthologist came in quick succession: *Tomie dePaola's Book of Christmas Carols*; *Tomie dePaola's Book of Poems*; *Tomie dePaola's Book of Bible Stories* (the Old Testament section of which was reissued in 1995 by popular demand as *Tomie dePaola's Book of the Old Testament*); *Joy to the World*; and *Hark! A Christmas Sampler*, written by Jane Yolen. Putting together these anthologies required the choosing or retelling of hundreds of selections; the creation of nearly one thousand full-color pieces of art; the preparation of grids for and the design of more than six hundred pages of text; the planning of front and back matter, endpapers, dust jackets, and book casings; and the coordination of all these elements through the production process. Not surprisingly, each anthology contains distinctive dePaola trademarks: luminescent use of color; a strong sense of balance between text, image, and white space; recurring folk motifs; and attention to the constrictions of bookmaking.

After a gap of nearly thirty years, another anthology recently appeared. *The Magical World of Strega Nona: A Treasury*—which, as mentioned earlier, includes both classic stories and new material—is ripe with dePaola's familiar and well-loved style. The visual themes and motifs he employs here add dimension to the book and give a special identity to his artwork—just as they do in all of his illustrations.

Michael Bird-Boy.

8

Informational Books

Most of dePaola's efforts in his early publishing years focused on illustrating other people's works, many of which were nonfiction, and which he did with great gusto. When looking chronologically at his work, one sees the beginnings of his current matured and familiar style, which includes a strong sense of design; the integration of animals as characters; touches of humor; cognizance of space; and decorative use of birds, stars, and suns.

Threading comedy and bits of whimsy into informational books has been one of dePaola's highly welcomed contributions to the genre, starting with his playful illustrations for his first book, Lisa Miller's *Sound*—although one unknown critic, dePaola well remembers, found the art "far too imaginative for a science book."[1] Today, though, teachers tell of finding young readers in hysterics over the amusing graphics scattered through his pages. In *Michael Bird-Boy*, dePaola tells of a young boy's concern about a black cloud that slowly appears over the countryside. The story brings understanding—and humor—to an environmental issue highly relevant today. The enlarged format and droll characters draw the reader to the pages.

"Charlie Needs a Cloak" is another example of a playful informational book. DePaola provides straightforward information about an everyday subject (making a cloak) while also lifting it above the ordinary through his witty, colorful drawings. By featuring one black-faced sheep—cantankerous

Sound.

but nevertheless enamored of Charlie—among a flock of otherwise identical sheep, dePaola creates a secondary character that works as a marvelous foil to Charlie and his cloak-making efforts. The sheep's expressive face, adorned with a beguiling set of frilly eyelashes, nudges the humor forward. The animal's elation in a bubble bath, embarrassment over its newly shorn body, determination to outpull Charlie in a tug-of-war over yarn, and numerous ploys to get the herder's attention resonate through the pictures. Meanwhile, the text concerns itself strictly with Charlie's labors. An early draft of this manuscript (then titled *Sebastian's Red Cloak*) shows the shepherd with a wife, but dePaola wisely decided that the story would be simpler—and stronger—if it revolved around just the shepherd and his sheep.[2] The decision also gives Charlie more of an any-age persona.

DePaola employs three noteworthy techniques in this book, which he has used successfully in various other titles: the introduction of the plot in the front matter, the use of sequence illustration, and the inclusion of visual extras.

Prior to the title page, villagers view Charlie in a ragged cloak, with the one black-faced sheep standing on a hillside above the rest of the flock. The text reads, "Charlie was a shepherd. He had a cozy house, a big hat, a crook, and a flock of fat sheep. But everyone said, . . ." On the next page the words "Charlie needs a cloak" complete the sentence and, in a nifty visual trick, provide the book's title.

The formal text, which begins, "Poor Charlie! He really needed a new cloak," is accompanied by an image showing the reason for the shepherd's condition—the black-faced sheep, contentedly chewing on Charlie's tattered garment. This scene also sets up the amusing ending: the sheep nibbling once more—this time on Charlie's brand-new cloak! It's a circular story, cleverly mapped out.

A fine example of a dePaola sequential-action scene takes place during the shearing. Across a double-page spread, the black-faced sheep apprehensively notes what is going on, races up a hill

Staged throughout the story, these three vignettes portray Charlie's ongoing plight with his sheep in *"Charlie Needs a Cloak."*

Charlie was a shepherd. He had a cozy house, a big hat, a crook, and a flock of fat sheep.

But everyone said,

The opening pages set the scene for *"Charlie Needs a Cloak."*

"CHARLIE NEEDS A CLOAK"

story and pictures by

Tomie dePaola

A small gray mouse carries away items in the lower portions of the double-page spreads in *"Charlie Needs a Cloak."*

with Charlie in pursuit, grapples with the determined shepherd, is overpowered and sheared, and is last seen with only his head sticking out of the bushes in embarrassment. This treatment of events heightens the humor and capsulizes the action.

The visual extra that dePaola includes in *"Charlie"* quietly unfolds in the lower portions of the double-page spreads. Perceptive viewers will spy a small gray mouse carrying away items often connected with Charlie's tasks (scissors during the sheep-shearing scene, red berries while Charlie dyes the wool, a ruler as Charlie measures the material). The shepherd, however, is completely oblivious to the creature's activities. At the story's close, the purpose of the mouse's maneuvers becomes clear—a small drawing reveals a cozy, tentlike structure that contains the mouse's completed cache.

The success of *"Charlie Needs a Cloak"* in 1973 encouraged dePaola to embark on other informational titles using a similar combination of fact and entertainment. *The Quicksand Book* also uses the front matter to lead into the story. From a ledge near her tree house, Jungle Girl merrily sails through the trees, only to have her vine break midswing—landing her in quicksand on the first page of the story. This device imaginatively opens the dialogue between Jungle Girl and Jungle Boy, who, in response to her call for help, blithely discusses the composition of quicksand and explains rescue procedures in the form of graphs and charts. Here, too, the illustrations feature a visual extra—this time a monkey setting up a table for tea. While the mouse incident in *"Charlie Needs a Cloak"* plays out separately from the primary action, dePaola incorporates this extra escapade into the plot of *Quicksand*. He brings the monkey into the main story, which culminates with Jungle Girl and the monkey enjoying tea and cakes, while Jungle Boy, now the one mired in the quicksand, shouts for assistance. The back of the dust jacket, however, assures young readers that all is well—the three characters perch happily together on a rope swing.

The Quicksand Book.

While dePaola's theatrical tendencies emerge in many of his works, his use of jungle foliage as a proscenium arch and his positioning of the action from a single point of view make this title an early and excellent example of that influence. This technique also allows for the smooth juxtaposition of characters and their dialogue exchange, and the placement of Jungle Boy's charts is remindful of the signboards used on the vaudeville stage. To avoid the stagnation that could result from the single viewpoint, the artist varies his scenes with the appearances of different animals (elephants, frogs, snakes, lions, turtles) and the monkey's tea-making antics.

In response to the often-asked question "Why a book on quicksand?" dePaola replied, "Growing up, I was infatuated with Tarzan movies, and as a small child, I was warned to stay away from a nearby brook—supposedly there was quicksand." He then quickly gave credit to a librarian who sent him a letter from her grandson asking for a book about quicksand. Obviously a dePaola fan, the boy (who called himself Stevem [*sic*]) seemed to think that if his grandmother was a librarian, then surely she knew the artist, and he suggested that she could have "Tomie dePaola write me one." DePaola quickly complied, and the book is dedicated to "Stevem and his grandmother." The research was difficult, dePaola related with a chuckle. "There is hardly anything available; I think I've written the definitive volume on the subject." When the book was released, the publisher received a telegram saying, "Stevem is ecstatic and is whipping up a batch of quicksand and the dedication has me swinging from a cloud."[3]

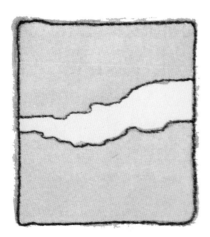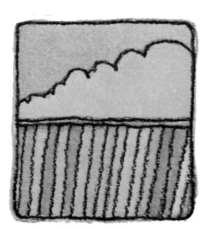

Clouds in *Michael Bird-Boy.*

DePaola includes directions for making quicksand in the book (which "Stevem" clearly followed). This kind of added touch is also found in the form of a silly bonus story starring a cloud in *The Cloud Book*, two popcorn recipes in *The Popcorn Book*, a list of cat facts in *The Kids' Cat Book*, and directions for creating a tree ornament in *The Family Christmas Tree Book*. The idea for including these extras derived from dePaola's interest as a child in making things.

In addition to the visual quips found in *The Popcorn Book*, humor is also embedded in the dialogue, as tousled-haired twins Tiny and Tony and their two identical cats sashay across the pages. While Tiny gives instructions for making popcorn, Tony supplies information about its history and relates anecdotes about its popularity—both of which are illustrated in balloons set off nicely from the ongoing story. When Tiny enthusiastically puts too many kernels into the pan, the twins experience an

DePaola and the old-fashioned popcorn machine in his studio.

explosion of popcorn in the kitchen, but no matter, because, as they say, "The best thing about popcorn is eating it!" As the popcorn tumbles up, down, and everywhere, children may notice a precursor to the flood of pasta in *Strega Nona*.

Harmony between picture and text is clearly in evidence in *Popcorn*, but once again it's the narrative element that makes these informational titles appealing to children and critically satisfying to adults. Also in evidence is dePaola's love of popcorn— as mentioned earlier, an old-fashioned popcorn machine sits at the ready in his studio!

The Popcorn Book.

9

Story Making: Patterns, Visual Themes, and Motifs

Writing stories in addition to illustrating them had always been a part of dePaola's career plan. His first writing attempt—and second publishing effort—was a simple original tale, *The Wonderful Dragon of Timlin*, which "quickly and quietly," according to dePaola, "went out of print." He followed that with a quartet of stories that are "best counted," dePaola laughingly acknowledged, "as learning experiences." Most of his energy during those early publishing years concentrated on sharpening his illustration techniques, but gradually tales of his own began taking shape in his head and on the page.

One early, well-received title was the poetic tale *When Everyone Was Fast Asleep*, derived from a time when dePaola, living in California, became interested in dream therapy. The story features a cat named Token who leads two small children into the enchanted world of night. The gauzy, pencil-shaded illustrations provide an ethereal look, and a larger-than-life Token brings cohesion to the somewhat slight story. The book merits notice as dePaola's first brush with poetry and, from the illustrative

Cats appear in many of dePaola's books (here, in *Fight the Night*).

In Andy & Sandy and the Big Talent Show, stage fright strikes Sandy.

side, for the way his images weave smoothly in and out in much the same way that mirages float through dreams.

In 1989 dePaola tackled a story about his own life in art. With *The Art Lesson* his intent was to show a young boy's confrontation with his art teacher and to provide, through his own childhood experience, a peek into children's early creativity. Two years later dePaola took another turn at art-themed story making—but with an entirely different approach—in *Bonjour, Mr. Satie*. Interpreting the masters is a graphic technique that dePaola enjoyed using, and one he ingeniously takes advantage of in this highly innovative story.

From start to finish, the book is handsomely presented, and its theme—that art is a matter of taste—is delivered with wit and aplomb. It's a theme that may well reverberate with children, especially those who doubt their own artistic abilities.

The jacket sets the scene. Mr. Satie, a debonair-looking cat, and his companion, Ffortusque Ffollet, Esq., a bespectacled, knickers-clad mouse, stroll the

Champs-Élysées. The Eiffel Tower and the Arc de Triomphe stand in the background. The book's front matter includes a postcard to Mr. Satie's niece and nephew, Rosalie and Conrad, informing them of Uncle Satie's arrival, and a two-page spread—which doubles as the title page—depicting Mr. Satie and Fortie as they journey by steamship, train, and taxi to Rosalie and Conrad's home in America.

Once there, Uncle Satie amuses Rosalie and Conrad with tales of his adventures in the French capital. One tale takes place in a Paris salon, where dePaola inserts a painting of a guitar-playing cat in the "blue period" style of Picasso's *The Old Guitarist*.[1] This witty depiction is especially fitting since the main character, Mr. Satie the cat, is an art critic. In another tale Uncle Satie successfully mediates an argument that breaks out at his friend Gertrude's Sunday-evening salon, which is attended by various luminaries of the 1920s Parisian art scene. The quarrel between Henri and Pablo centers on whose paintings are the best, but soon everyone enters the fray.[2] After careful scrutiny Mr. Satie declares (in a splendid piece of wordplay by dePaola) that "the contest is a draw."

Bonjour, Mr. Satie.

The real-world characters are aptly portrayed, and while younger children may not readily recognize such names as "Pablo," "Henri," "Gertrude," and "Alice," that's not important. Some youngsters will find their curiosities satisfied by perceptive teachers and other adults; others may remember these names years later and make the connection; still others will just enjoy the tale. And when the battle royal breaks out over whose pictures are the best (Pablo's or Henri's), children will identify with the crisis—and adults will find an opportunity for discussion concerning people's taste in art. In Mr. Satie's words: "I have concluded that to compare Henri's paintings with Pablo's would be to compare apples with oranges. Both are delicious but *taste* totally different."

For the older reader *Bonjour, Mr. Satie* can be an insightful introduction to the real people portrayed in the story, who are partially identified on the back flap with first names and last initials (Claude M., Josephine B., Isadora D., Zelda F., Ernest H., etc.).[3] The book also provides a wider understanding of the early-twentieth-century Parisian art scene, and of the relationships among—and even beyond—these figures. For example, Picasso was a close friend of the artist Georges Braque, who, though not included in the book, painted *Still Life with Score by Satie* in honor of his friend, the composer Erik Satie, whose name dePaola gave to his real-life Abyssinian cat—and to his main character.[4]

This illustration from *Marianna May and Nursey* showcases many of dePaola's recurring themes—a cat, a heart, a white bird, and the creation of art.

Bonjour, Mr. Satie offers a somewhat sophisticated look at artistic endeavors; it's about accomplished artists who have already proven their worth. However, it also echoes dePaola's deep feelings about art, about the need for individual expression, and about the pleasure found in drawing and painting (also addressed in *The Art Lesson*). And the book is another example of dePaola leading the way. After the publication of *Bonjour, Mr. Satie*, several other illustrators followed his lead, inserting famous artists into their books.[5]

Throughout his storytelling dePaola appreciates the necessity of a strong narrative thread, especially in a wordless book, as seen in *Pancakes for Breakfast*. The plot concerns a country lady's attempts to make a pancake breakfast, which is humorously hindered by a scarcity of ingredients and her pets' gluttonous hunger. While words do appear in a hand-lettered recipe, the pictures carry the story: a clock and a changing sky signal the passing hours, thought bubbles reveal what the woman anticipates (a stack of pancakes dripping with butter), and changing facial expressions provide ongoing amusement. The use of a long horizontal format enhances the simple, linear story line.

Bill and Pete.

Bill and Pete to the Rescue.

A horizontal orientation is also employed in dePaola's Bill and Pete stories, which now number three: *Bill and Pete, Bill and Pete Go Down the Nile,* and *Bill and Pete to the Rescue.* The droll escapades of Bill the crocodile and his friend, a bird named Pete, stretch out across each spread. The artist sustains visual interest with funny scenes of grinning white crocodile teeth and a man's spotted shorts, all in sync with the unfolding melodrama. Other deft touches include visual clues to a mystery, hilarious malapropisms, and Bill's fear that his missing father is now a suitcase. DePaola takes every opportunity to embellish and enlarge his text visually. "Pictures can do the writing," dePaola asserted. "They do more than help the story; they amplify it. There must be room in the story line for the creation of images that invite the child's imagination to wander. The other world of things unsaid and unexplained is what I try to find, see, and portray."

While in some ways, dePaola admitted, writing his own stories gave him more freedom for visual play, he also found working with another writer to be an exciting challenge. In the world of collaboration, dePaola has enjoyed the company of top writers in the field, including Jean Fritz, Patricia MacLachlan, Jane Yolen, Steven Kroll, Daniel Pinkwater, and Nancy Willard. He even reinterpreted Sarah Josepha

Hale's 1830 poem "Mary Had a Little Lamb," taking the classic poem beyond the familiar. He includes all six verses, rarely done, and weaves them into a full-blown, imaginative, and highly visual story. Beneath opening notes about the poem's background, he imagines Hale's home in Newport, New Hampshire. Then, on the title page, he portrays the woman at her writing desk, looking down at a lamb pull toy as though it were the source of her inspiration. Music is included in addition to the lyrics; typical New England backgrounds, the homespun look of the costumes, and other details also befit the poem.

He followed her to school one day—
That was against the rule,

Mary Had a Little Lamb.

But the collaborator with whom dePaola has most often shared the title page is Tony Johnston, whom he calls a "dream to work with; she leaves huge textual gaps for me as illustrator to fill in." In *The Quilt Story*, for example, a frontier mother stitches a quilt for her daughter, Abigail, which the girl uses for a gown, as a tea party tablecloth, and to keep warm on the windswept prairie. When her family moves farther west, Abigail finds the quilt comforting. Eventually the keepsake is

Rounded images nestled in the artwork bring pleasing symmetry to the page in *The Quilt Story.*

put into the attic, where it lies forgotten until another young girl, generations later, finds it badly in need of repair. Her mother patches the holes and puts in fresh padding, making the quilt whole and beautiful once again. And when this family relocates, the quilt comforts this girl too, in her new home. DePaola included two poignant images that give extra dimension to the story. When the second girl discovers the old quilt, readers will notice a framed picture of young Abigail and her cloth doll among the attic clutter. Then, in the penultimate image, the modern-day girl is seen in bed, snuggled under the quilt; at her side is the cloth doll, and above her bed hangs Abigail's portrait—connections across the ages.

Another dePaola collaborator was Nancy Willard. Illustrations for her quirky tale *The Mountains of Quilt* deserve close inspection, as they come nearest to the colors and shapes found in much of dePaola's non-book art. While familiar dePaola elements are present—floating stars, strong curved lines, pleasing shapes—the total look is different. Here he employs the entire page, often encircling Willard's text and placing small, fanciful figures in soft colors against white space, broken up with fluid, sketchy lines. The result is whimsical and entirely in keeping with Willard's wry tale. DePaola clearly had fun with the theme, designing the quilts in more fanciful ways than in *The Quilt Story* or *The Night Before Christmas*.

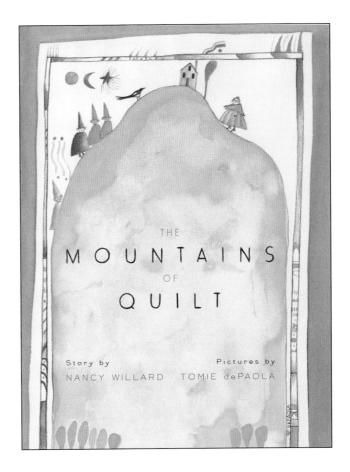

Quilt-like patterning makes an appearance in dePaola's non-book art, shown here hanging in his home studio.

Recurring themes in dePaola's work include rabbits (TOP CENTER, *Quiet*); hearts (UPPER LEFT, *The Cat on the Dovrefell*); cats (UPPER RIGHT, *Guess Who's Coming to Santa's for Dinner?*); and stars, moons, and again, rabbits (BOTTOM TWO IMAGES, *Strega Nona*).

Quilts, pancakes, popcorn—what is important to dePaola often surfaces in his story making. The recurrence of certain visual themes, patterns, symbols, and motifs is part of what identifies dePaola's work, and makes his books so special. Partially because of these elements, the artist is recognized far beyond the children's book world by book collectors, seekers of religious titles, devotees of folkloric objets d'art, and appreciators of whimsy. While these aficionados find their own connections to the white birds, hearts, stars, moons, terriers, rabbits, and cats that grace dePaola's pages—sometimes as decorations, sometimes as integral parts of his illustrations—dePaola says that for him these symbols have both an artistic and a personal significance.

DePaola with several of his beloved terriers, ABOVE, which often featured in his artwork (LEFT, in *Quiet*).

The Story of the Three Wise Kings.

So closely is dePaola associated with these symbols that when they aren't included, readers are likely to note their absence. Yet their inclusion has also brought reproof that his illustrations "all look alike." That criticism may come, in part, from a wrongful notion that these figures appear in all of dePaola's books. In fact, they aren't found in his autobiographical tales at all, and are never used indiscriminately. "I include them when the story calls for a highly stylized technique, such as in *Francis, the Poor Man of Assisi*; when there is enough latitude for a visual joke, such as in *Marianna May and Nursey*; or when there is room for graphic elaboration, such as in *The Story of the Three Wise Kings*. There I deliberately painted the Mother and Child, for example, in a traditional Romanesque-style pose referred to as 'Seat of Wisdom, Throne of Justice.'"

DePaola's real-life menagerie of animals changed over the years, in tandem with the animals that appear in his books. Early in his career dePaola had a schnauzer, seen romping around the background of *Finders Keepers, Losers Weepers*. Later he owned cats—Satie among them—that enjoyed starring roles in *The Kids' Cat Book* and *Bonjour, Mr. Satie*. Airedales are spotlighted in *Tomie dePaola's Mother Goose*, and his onetime Welsh terriers make appearances in multiple books, including the Barker Twins series. And the rabbits? "Well," dePaola remarked with a grin, "they just show up."

White birds have undoubtedly become the motif most associated with dePaola, and he used them liberally. Although the white bird in its current form didn't appear in dePaola's work until the 1970s, birds as decorative objects can be found even in early books such as *Sound* (1965). Through the years their shapes and colorings have been refined, and now readers—especially children—often seek them out as assurance that a title is indeed a dePaola book.

One of Tomie's many white birds, from *Michael Bird-Boy.*

As for hearts, dePaola related, they "crept into my art years ago and have stayed there out of habit." During the flower-child era of the 1960s, his apprenticeship with liturgical artist Corita Kent was often marked with heart decorations.[6] It seemed natural, dePaola said, to incorporate the heart shape into many of his pictures and into his signature. At times he had even used it to frame an image on the page, and beginning in 1982, a small heart almost always appears on his cover art. Then, in the midst of a three-hour autographing session at a bookstore in Denver, he stopped signing his last name. Sometime later at an American Library Association conference, in what dePaola described as a pivotal moment in his career, he decided to adopt the combined heart-Tomie pen stroke as his "official" signature.

Traditions were important to dePaola, so it is no surprise to find images of his familiar characters woven into many of his books. Charlie from *"Charlie Needs a Cloak"* has become, as has Strega Nona, somewhat of a dePaola icon. The stalwart shepherd can be found tucked into a variety of the artist's books—as a lamb's doll in *Haircuts for the Woolseys*, as a traveler in *The Cloud Book*, as a dream image in *Songs of the Fog Maiden*, and more.

Neither is Strega Nona shy about demanding her share of recognition. One can find her in pictures on the wall in both *The Wuggie Norple Story* and *I Love You, Mouse*, as a memento of the grown-up Tomie's work in *The Art Lesson*, and in *Tomie dePaola's Mother Goose*. Also interesting are the precursors that appear in the

Strega Nona's Magic Ring,
ABOVE and BELOW.

second book dePaola illustrated, for example—*The Tiger and the Rabbit* by Pura Belpré—that includes a Strega Nona look-alike.

The positioning of the human hand is another recurring device in dePaola's books. This can be attributed to the influence of pre-Renaissance art, where the hand is often given visual prominence. At times dePaola used the technique to help portray character (Big Anthony), provide expression (*Days of the Blackbird*), energize the action (*Look and Be Grateful*), or direct the eye (*The Quilt Story*). Especially striking examples can be noted on the cover of *Francis, the Poor Man of Assisi*, and in the spread showing cookie baking from *An Early American Christmas*.

DePaola often included visual jokes in his work. Examples range from a boy reading a magic book upside down in Patricia MacLachlan's *Moon, Stars, Frogs, and Friends*; to the appearance of a medieval bookmobile in *The Knight and the Dragon*; to drawings of Puss in Boots, the Owl and the Pussycat, and other literary cats in *The Kids' Cat Book*; to the variety of Mother Goose characters tucked into the backgrounds of *Jack*; and the picture of a suitcase labeled "Dad" in *Bill and Pete*. All

display dePaola's mischievous joy in graphic jokes. Further evidence can be found in a note accompanying a Kerlan-held early sketch for *Big Anthony and the Magic Ring* (now called *Strega Nona's Magic Ring*) that reads, "Big Anthony—leaning like man in Millet's *The Angelus*."[7] Of these sly visual nods, dePaola commented, "If readers see them, that's great—and many kids relish finding them. If not, that is okay too; I know they are there."

The artist's thespian predilections, carried through from childhood and extended by his teaching and work both onstage and behind the curtain, carry heavy influence. In fact, he recommended that anyone interested in illustrating children's books have an "avid love of theater." As he pointed out, "An illustrator must cast the play, costume the characters, plan their entrances and exits, design the setting, and move the main action forward—all while not losing sight of the overall plot." One can find hints of this fondness for theater in many of dePaola's books—backdrops resembling stage sets; action that takes place front and center, seen from one perspective; his penchant for introducing characters by placing them in windows, which focuses attention like a spotlight does onstage. This theatrical influence can be seen as children put on a Nativity play in *The Christmas Pageant*, when Old Mother Hubbard's story is played

Old Mother Hubbard
Went to the cupboard
To fetch her poor dog a bone;
But when she got there
The cupboard was bare,
And so the poor dog had none.

The Comic Adventures of Old Mother Hubbard and Her Dog.

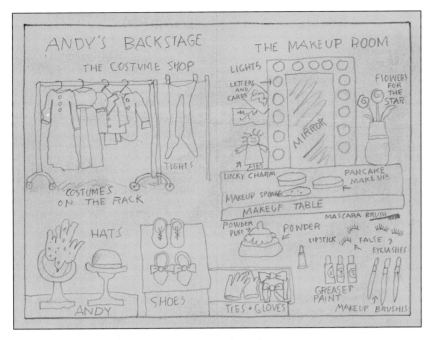

Endpapers in *Andy & Sandy and the Big Talent Show.*

out as a theatrical production in *The Comic Adventures of Old Mother Hubbard and Her Dog*, and when Jack and Jill appear as marionette figures in *Tomie dePaola's Mother Goose*. In another recent example the endpapers for *Andy & Sandy and the Big Talent Show* ready young readers for the tale to come with sketches of backstage scenes.

The window is also an important motif in dePaola's work. On the first page of *The Knight and the Dragon*, the knight appears in the window of a medieval tower, while the dragon peers from the rounded opening of his cave; Mary is first glimpsed through an open barn door in *Mary Had a Little Lamb*; Strega Nona often oversees the goings-on of Calabria from the window of her small house; and on the back jacket of *Tomie dePaola's Front Porch Tales*, dePaola himself shouts a greeting from a barn window. Not only does this device bring attention to the character, but it also draws young readers into the action and the tale within.

Mary Had a Little Lamb.

DePaola was one of the first to use the front matter of a book to tantalize his readers. Prime examples include *Watch Out for the Chicken Feet in Your Soup*, in which Joey warns his friend Eugene about his eccentric grandmother even before the title page, and Elizabeth Winthrop's *Maggie and the Monster*, where, on the half-title page, a figure stealthily enters an open door—followed on the title page by a huge shadow skulking behind the big-eared, plaid-dressed green monster. Sometimes, as in *Days of the Blackbird*, dePaola used the title page to place the story geographically, while in *Bonjour, Mr. Satie* the journey from Paris to Rosalie and Conrad's home skillfully unfolds on the title-page spread. And on the title page of *Tom*, dePaola introduces his characters through photograph-like images, bringing about a nostalgic look.

Innovation has been a hallmark of dePaola's work in a variety of ways. In many of his books readers can find sources, a note on the evolution of a tale, or information about how dePaola became aware of a story. Although today it is common practice to include extras like these, it was not earlier in his career, when he provided source material for 1980s titles such as *The Lady of Guadalupe* and *The Legend of the Indian Paintbrush*. Dialogue makes up the complete narrative in *Watch Out for the Chicken Feet in Your Soup*, an approach that was certainly unique at the time of publication. Also innovative is his use of sequence illustration; one scene in *Mary Had a Little Lamb* (see image at left) cleverly emphasizes the line "And everywhere that Mary went, the lamb was sure to go" by showing the lamb listening to Mary read in the attic, keeping her company in the kitchen, and sleeping at the foot of her bed—all on one spread. The artist is quick to assert, however, that he did not invent this device; its use can be traced to examples from art history, such as the work of Brueghel the Elder and the Bayeux Tapestry.[8]

Where does all this creativity come from? "When you've been in publishing as long as I have," dePaola remarked, "you try to vary your work to keep it fresh, while still keeping within your own style." Having been in the profession for a long time, "I've seen a lot of changes," he said. What he didn't always see in new children's book creators was "a sense of their own vision. In some ways there has been a loss of story—too many picture books today are merely portfolios of paintings. On the other hand there is much for teachers and parents to choose from. Those looking to share books with children have a nearly endless variety of art styles, techniques, mediums, and palettes available—a great difference from what I had as a child."

"Tomie, Where Do You Get Your Ideas?"

by Tomie dePaola

One of the first questions I get asked by children and grown-ups is, "Where do you get your ideas?" The answer I give is "I don't really know. I guess they ultimately come from inside myself." All my characters seem to be parts of me, even Helga and Strega Nona. But what releases these ideas and characters is still a mystery to me. It can be one of those "light bulb" situations like in the comic strips, or just plain tedious coaxing. Sometimes it's a piece of music, a painting, an old photograph, or even a cup of coffee.

Marianna May came from looking at an old photograph of my mother all dressed up with a huge bow in her hair; *The Night of Las Posadas* from watching this beautiful Mexican tradition carried out when I visited New Mexico one Christmas; and *The Hunter and the Animals* from a day when I was home, leafing through Tamas Hofer's *Hungarian Folk Art.*⁹

I was simply struck by this reproduction of a Hungarian painted-wood panel—by its intricacy of pattern. It kept going through my mind, and eventually I used it as the basis for a wordless story about a lost hunter who is rescued by the forest animals and in thanksgiving breaks his gun in half. To the stylized patterns I added my own measure of color and detail through the acorn-laden trees and the band of animals that peek through the foliage.

But whenever an idea or character is ready to jump out, I'd better be ready to grab it. Then it's just good old-fashioned hard work to take the idea and make it work. No magic involved, just hard work, some luck, a good editor, and a lot of love on my part.

When I was in Italy for my first Bologna book fair, I met Leo Lionni, which was a genuine thrill. Over dinner one night he lowered his voice and asked me, "Do you ever worry you don't have any more ideas?" It was wonderful to hear that fear—which many an author or artist has—expressed. "Of course I do," I told him. "But I have a trick. I always try to come up with a new project before I finish the one I'm working on. Sort of like sourdough bread—you take a little dough to start your new batch."

Marianna May and Nursey.

Then, too, I try to stay open to ideas. When children ask me, which they often do, where I get my ideas, I tell them, from everywhere. It's a question of being open, receptive—like an empty cup. Of course, not every idea is a good one. The boring ones usually go quietly away, and it helps to have good editorial feedback.

The Knight and the Dragon actually came from a reading-promotion poster I had done for the American Library Association. It had hung on my studio wall for months, when suddenly a kernel of an idea popped out, which eventually became the story and art you see today.

As for the Bill and Pete stories, their genesis is an article I read in *National Geographic* about the natural symbiotic relationship between the crocodile and the Egyptian plover. The whole idea amused me, and I began to create some stories about these two unlikely friends. Originally there were three individual tales, but as my editor and I worked through the idea, it seemed better to integrate them into one story. *Bill and Pete* was the result, and when it proved popular, I wrote two more!

10
Publishing History

By the late seventies, dePaola had firmly established his stature in the children's literature field, and book ideas kept bubbling up from his ever-creative mind. Reminiscing about his career, however, he quickly gave credit to those who were there early on when advice and help were needed. Connecting with Florence Alexander, he admitted, helped his career take the decided turn in the direction that he had long wanted to go. As often happens, this bit of fate came about through an odd chain of events. DePaola came to know Blanche Gregory, a literary agent who handled adult authors, through a mutual friend. Gregory had decided to expand her business and represent a few illustrators, and at a cocktail party she suggested that dePaola get a portfolio ready for review.[1] Shortly after that, however, Gregory was elected president of the Agents' Guild, a time-heavy commitment that precluded taking on any new clients.[2] DePaola received the bad news when he went to Gregory's Manhattan office to show his portfolio. In a burst of kindness Gregory called Alexander, who was an artists' agent, asking if she might be interested in this young talent. "Sure," dePaola remembered Alexander telling Gregory, "if he can get down to my office by noon." To echo Strega Nona, the rest is history.

At that time dePaola's teaching load at Newton College in the Boston area allowed him the flexibility to live in Manhattan, where he was close to publishers. Teaching gave him a small income as well as classroom experience, which proved to be especially important: "My efforts to verbalize my thoughts to students," he said, "made me internalize

Michael Bird-Boy.

Quiet.

my own work and philosophy about art to myself."

As his reputation grew, so did his output. And in the mid-1960s, dePaola's own writing took seed. Bernice Kohn Hunt,[3] according to dePaola, was an early mentor. Not only was her book *Sound* his first illustration assignment, but she was also helpful when he wrote his first story—the somewhat slight but nevertheless sweet *Wonderful Dragon of Timlin.*

Then, in the late 1960s, with his work gaining recognition and with the support of his agent, dePaola felt free to head for California. He spent more than four years in the City by the Bay. They were busy years, as he recalls, and the record proves it. He produced nearly thirty books. Although most were written by other people, he authored six of them himself. He worked with editors Jeanne Vestal (Lippincott), Mary Russell (Bobbs-Merrill), and Eunice Holsaert (Hawthorn) on various projects. "They were each extremely helpful and willing to give time and attention to a young writer and illustrator," he recalled.

Prentice-Hall editor Ellen Roberts, who shepherded *Strega Nona* from that doodle on the drawing pad to a Caldecott Honor Book, and Holsaert, who had moved to Holiday House, proved to be especially strong guiding forces. When dePaola moved back to the East Coast in 1971, Holsaert encouraged him to draw from the memories of his childhood to

130

write his own stories. In an ironic turn of events, after helping him with the early stages of writing *Nana Upstairs & Nana Downstairs*, Holsaert declined the manuscript when it was finished. DePaola then submitted it to Barbara Lucas at Putnam, where the book was completed; it garnered great reviews and became an immediate success with children and critics alike.

When Lucas moved on to Harcourt, dePaola continued his work with her, publishing books such as *The Clown of God* and *Helga's Dowry*. Margaret Frith, who had been an associate editor at Coward-McCann, moved into Lucas's spot at Putnam, and she and dePaola began what became a successful, longtime relationship there. *Bill and Pete*, published in 1978, was their first of many collaborations.

In time Lucas left Harcourt, and dePaola began working with editor Maria Modugno there; he also developed a close working connection with John and Kate Briggs and editor Margery Cuyler at Holiday House. "With *Quicksand*," dePaola remembered, "Margery encouraged me to be as humorous as possible—to just take it and run. We also shared a strong interest in religious themes. Holiday House allowed me to do *Francis, the Poor Man of Assisi* and *The Lady of Guadalupe* the way I wanted to do them, without forcing them into a commercial mode." It was under the Holiday House imprint that dePaola published many of his Christmas and religious titles, as well as popular books such as *Mary Had a Little Lamb* and *The Hunter and the Animals*.[4] The latter, a wordless book with a distinct anti-hunting message, elicited a bit of controversy from gun owners.

Brushes with censorship, however, have been few; likewise, dePaola came through another publishing hazard—the reviewing process—more or less unscathed. That is not to say that he hasn't suffered a few slings and arrows. In reviewing *Francis, the Poor Man of Assisi* for *The New York Times Book Review*, Mary Gordon, an author of books for adults, said she longed for a portrayal of Francis that was "a bit more ragged, a bit wilder, that the wolf looked a little less tame, the stigmata a bit more bloody." In reviewing *Quicksand*, a critic suggested that Jungle Girl (rather than Jungle Boy) should have been the rescuer; and in *The New York Times Book Review*, David Macaulay called *The Art Lesson* "mediocre and self-indulgent," a lone negative voice on the highly regarded title.[5] More often than not, however, the reviews have been in dePaola's favor, and he has racked up more stars, best books, children's choices, notables, and generally outstanding reviews than most of his contemporaries. His work has also generated numerous articles, interviews, and profiles; and he has gained more kudos, awards, recognitions, and honors than are feasible to list here (a chronological list appears in the appendix).

When technological advances in the printing industry allowed publishers to drop the preseparated art process and reproduce illustrations directly from the original artwork, dePaola's work, along with other artists', could be better appreciated through a truer representation of colors and more defined line work.[6] This allowed him to use the palette's full range and to experiment with color, shape, and texture. He could choose a style—from painterly to comic book to folk art—that fit the text, rather than be bound by the restrictions of reproduction.

DePaola's publishing relationship with Holiday House ended only when he

signed an exclusive global agreement with Putnam. There were exceptions; according to dePaola, Frith and Putnam were very understanding about allowing him some freedom with the contract. Nevertheless, the global agreement, the first in the industry for a children's book illustrator, is one that dePaola was proud of because, he felt, "it brought recognition and importance to all the children's book field."

In 1989, as part of this agreement, Putnam launched a new imprint called Whitebird Books.[7] DePaola served as creative director of the line, which featured less familiar folktales from around the world, paired with established writers and lesser-known artists. While a few titles carried dePaola's name as author or illustrator, those that did not were often lost in the huge number of multicultural folktales and stories that flooded the market in the 1990s. Ultimately, the imprint was lost as well; it was disbanded in 1994.

In 1997, Putnam became part of Penguin Putnam, but the financial dealings at the top did not affect the long affiliation between dePaola and Frith. While they differed at times about details, their almost daily communications by phone, by email, and in person continued to bring about numerous remarkable books.

Around the time that Penguin merged with Random House, the thirty-year contract with dePaola came to an end. Then Frith retired from her longtime position as editor of children's books, and dePaola worked on multiple titles with Nancy Paulsen. He also decided to test the waters with other publishing companies. Doug Whiteman, whom dePaola knew from Whiteman's days as president of the children's section of Putnam, was about to begin his own literary agency, and dePaola signed with Whiteman to be his agent.

Strega Nona and the Twins.

Hearing the news of dePaola's new arrangement with the Whiteman Agency, Simon & Schuster stepped forward, choosing editor Emma Ledbetter, followed by Kristin Ostby, and art director Laurent Linn as a viable team to work with dePaola.

Both reissued backlist titles and brand-new stories were rolling off the presses.

DePaola continued to be busy. One fine example of his latest work is *In a Small Kingdom*, a modern fairy tale written by dePaola but illustrated in a debut appearance by Doug Salati. The story tells of a magical robe gone missing, until mutual love between the village people and a young prince finally brings peace. Salati's warm, dusky colors, smooth rendition of characters, and prudent use of the page gather readers and listeners to this evocative story about the power of love. In a heartfelt tribute to his mentor, Salati tucked an image of dePaola into a background scene.

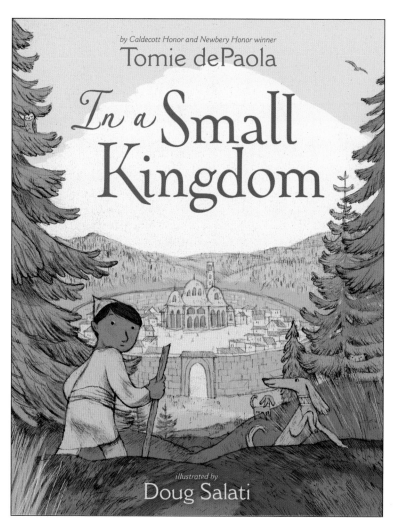

In a Small Kingdom, with a guest appearance by dePaola himself, BELOW, in the upper-left corner.

Amah gathered those who could sew. They sewed and sewed, but still fragments were missing.

"Tell everyone to bring a piece of fabric that is precious to them," said Amah. "If they give lovingly, the Robe can be completed."

"My, oh my," the grandfather said.
"Everything is in such a hurry.

ABOVE and BELOW,
two double-page spreads
from *Quiet*.

Another recent release is *Quiet*, written and illustrated by dePaola, a picture book that suggests the pleasure in finding a corner to pause, think, and muse about everyday life. Here two children and their grandfather enjoy a morning walk together. While coming across frogs jumping, birds flapping, and bees buzzing, they also discover the pleasures of just being quiet, as do the animals and birds. DePaola's softened colors and carefully paced action support this simple, strong story.

"Let us be quiet, like all our friends.
Quiet and still."

In Cheryl Klein's *Wings*, dePaola cleverly showcases the acrobatics of a bright pink bird's first flight. Single words on each page—for example, *clings*, *flings*, and *springs*—provide great leeway to depict the action, and the artist takes full advantage with portrayals bursting with expression and energy.

DePaola continued to explore beyond the picture book format as well. His Andy & Sandy series, co-written with Jim Lewis (of Muppets fame) and illustrated by dePaola, is drawing in emerging readers, while Ready-to-Read stories featuring Strega Nona and geared toward particular reading levels have quickly found their mark. A new board book developed especially for parents, written by Phyllis Grann and illustrated by dePaola—*I Will Talk to You, Little One*—encourages "talking to your baby from infancy."[8]

Haircuts for Little Lambs (previously titled *Haircuts for the Woolseys*) join redesigned and restored editions of *Fight the Night*; *Michael Bird-Boy*; *Andy, That's My Name*; and *Oliver Button Is a Sissy*; all are relevant and meaningful and substantiate dePaola's always expanding reputation.

Wings.

Andy & Sandy's Anything Adventure.

Quiet

TOMIE dePAOLA

11
Creating the Book

DePaola's onetime casual remark that Strega Nona went from doodle pad to book might give the impression that his illustrative process happened overnight. Nothing could be further from the truth. "Even before the writing begins," dePaola maintained, "a picture book sits in my head for long periods of time. Then, depending on its complexity and what else is happening in my life, it might take months to create. I often work on several books at once—while I'm checking galleys for a spring book, for instance, I might be working on the art scheduled for a fall release, and also sketching out ideas for a future title."

As to where to start, dePaola explained, "My first impulse is to begin with the pictures, but I restrain myself: I thoroughly believe that story comes first." As to what makes a good story for children? DePaola responded quickly: "The same things that make a good story for adults: complexity, plot, character development, suspense, drama, humor, sadness. The only difference is that in a children's book, you have fewer words and more pictures."

Furthermore, he explained, "Text space can be limiting; a big idea might have to be compressed into a single sentence, while too much text could squeeze out the art." Another factor he considered was the way words sound, because a picture book is likely to be read aloud. When the text was completed, dePaola then began preparing sketches, which often looked like doodles because, he claimed, "if my drawings are too complete, the final artwork dies." Actual drawings for a thirty-two-page picture book could take from six weeks up to three months to complete, while an extended book, such as *Mother Goose*, took several years from creative seed to finished product. When asked about his preferred art approach, dePaola firmly stated that it was important to wisely choose the medium and technique most appropriate to the story.

Following are the stages dePaola went through to bring his last picture book, the *New York Times* best-selling *Quiet*, to fruition. DePaola's willingness to allow sketches, changes, rough drafts, and final copy to be reproduced here permits a glimpse of the creativity, the work, the care, the detail, the time, and the love that went into just one of his books.

"Look at the birds, flying so fast." the grandfather said.

"And that dog is running after a ball." said the girl.

"I see a frog jumping high, into the pond," said the boy.

"And a dragonfly zooming over the water." (girl)

My, oh my." grandfather said, "Everything is in such a hurry. Busy as busy can be."

"Even the trees are waving their leaves." (boy)

"Why don't we sit here, you next to me. Let's not be so busy." (G.F.)

"The birds are just, like us. They are taking a rest, singing their song." (girl)

"The dog is ~~asleep~~ tired out, I think he's dreaming. from his play." (B)

"The frog is just sitting and blinking". (B)

The dragonfly has stopped, too! ½ (G)

So, just let our thoughts fly through our minds, like the birds. Let us be quiet, like all our friends." (GF)

"Quiet and still is such a nice thing to be."

"I can think, when I'm quiet." (G)

"I can see, when I am still." (B)

"To be quiet and still - what a special thing." (GF)

The handwritten first draft of the manuscript for *Quiet*.

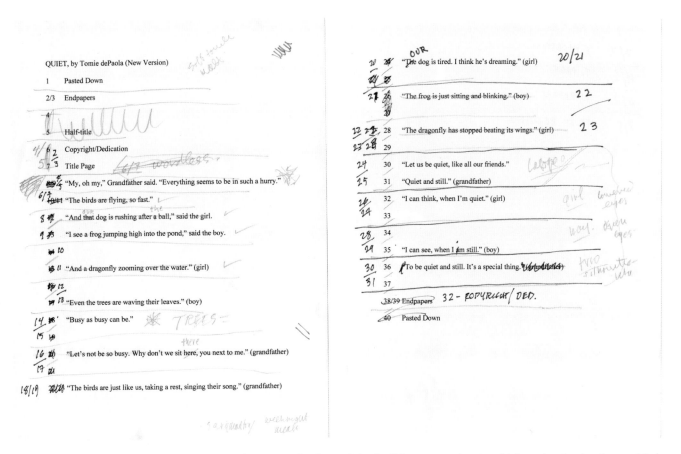

QUIET, by Tomie dePaola (New Version)

1   Pasted Down

2/3   Endpapers

4

5   Half-title

6   Copyright/Dedication

7   Title Page

"My, oh my," Grandfather said. "Everything seems to be in such a hurry."

"The birds are flying, so fast."

"And that dog is rushing after a ball," said the girl.

"I see a frog jumping high into the pond," said the boy.

"And a dragonfly zooming over the water." (girl)

"Even the trees are waving their leaves." (boy)

"Busy as busy can be."

"Let's not be so busy. Why don't we sit here, you next to me." (grandfather)

"The birds are just like us, taking a rest, singing their song." (grandfather)

20   "The dog is tired. I think he's dreaming." (girl)   20/21

21   "The frog is just sitting and blinking." (boy)   22

28   "The dragonfly has stopped beating its wings." (girl)   23

29

30   "Let us be quiet, like all our friends."

31   "Quiet and still." (grandfather)

32   "I can think, when I'm quiet." (girl)

33

34

35   "I can see, when I am still." (boy)

36   "To be quiet and still. It's a special thing." (grandfather)

37

38/39 Endpapers   32 - COPYRIGHT/DED.

40   Pasted Down

A later, near-final typed draft of the manuscript, in which pagination has been added. Some lines shifted slightly (namely, the opening of the book) and word choice was tweaked a bit, but overall the final manuscript did not change much from Tomie's original vision.

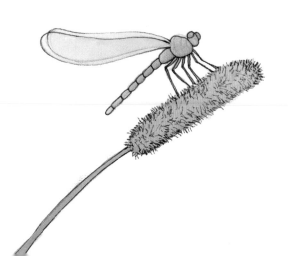

Quiet
Tomie dePaola
Simon & Schuster Books for Young Readers
New York   London   Toronto   Sydney   New Delhi

"Look at the birds, flying so fast," Grandfather said.

"And that dog is rushing after a ball," said the girl.

"I see a frog jumping high, into the pond," said the boy.

"And a dragonfly zooming over the water."

"Even the trees are waving their leaves."

"My, oh my," Grandfather said. "Everything is in such a hurry.

Busy as busy can be."

"Why don't we sit here, you next to me. Let's not be so busy."

"The birds are just like us. They are taking a rest, singing their song."

"The dog is tired. I think he's dreaming."

"The frog is just sitting and blinking."

"The dragonfly has stopped beating its wings."

"Let us be quiet, like all our friends.
Let our thoughts fly through our minds like birds,"
Grandfather said.

"Quiet and still."

"I can think, when I'm quiet."

"I can see, when I'm still."

To be quiet and still is a special thing.

The final manuscript, copyedited and circulated to the design department for placement in layouts.

141

Early in the art process, dePaola began with character design and development sketches for the girl, the boy, and their grandfather. Initially, the grandfather appeared younger and wore a cap instead of a brimmed hat.

For the spread on pages 6–7 (text: "The birds are flying so fast"), dePaola sketched a rough scene, working out composition of the characters and their placement within the spread.

As dePaola homed in on the composition, he began to add more detail to the scene and to toy further with the characters' appearances, clothing, and positioning.

Before working on final illustrations, dePaola experimented with various color palettes and hues.

The final painting for pages 6–7.

The final layout of pages 6–7, with text, as it appears in the finished book.

12
DePaola's Non-Book Art

Bins full of small still-life paintings, shadow boxes containing bits of realia, and files brimming with costumes and scenery sketches offer another side to dePaola's artistic inclinations. While in his beginning years as an artist he painted large, liturgical pieces—he was one of a handful of people working in contemporary liturgical art, and his talents were in great demand—he stopped doing that to fulfill his many book obligations. For a change of pace from his illustration work, however, dePaola had occasionally returned to this venue, finding, he said, satisfaction in both much smaller and much larger canvases, and in lighter and heavier palettes.

These pieces found a summer home at Cove Gallery in Wellfleet, Massachusetts, for several years, where a combined exhibit of dePaola's illustration and non-book art, curated by Sherry Litwack, drew large crowds during the tourist-heavy summer on Cape Cod. And over a two-year period, Colby-Sawyer College featured both dePaola's illustration and fine art work

"The Being of God Is the Beauty of All There Is"—self-portrait
oil on canvas
36" x 29 3/4"
1956

Big Whitebird Tower
acrylic on canvas
3' x 3'
2002

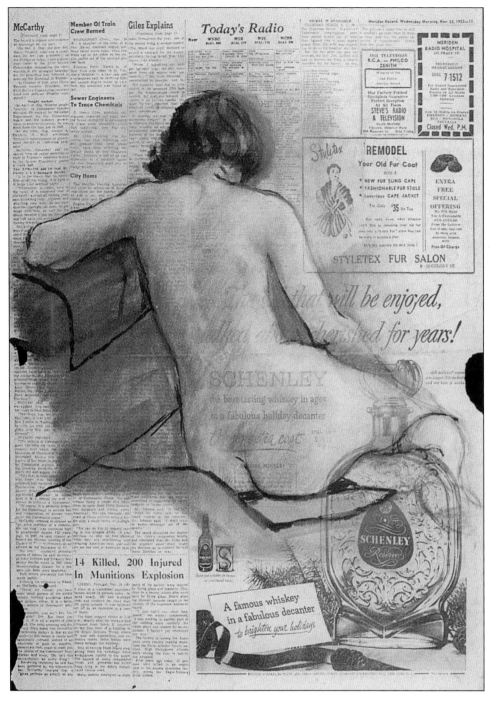

Life Study, Pratt Institute
pastel and ink on newspaper
22 3/4" x 16 1/2"
circa 1953

from across five decades in two exhibitions collectively called *Tomie dePaola: Then and Now.*

Among other projects, he had also designed fabric for a weaving studio, made vestments for the chapel in the Île-de-France, created the architectural drawings for his present studio, and sculpted masks used in the stage production of *The Clown of God.*

"In order to keep my picture book art fresh," dePaola said in a 1992 interview, "I've been making pencil and watercolor drawings and large splashy paintings on paper. One of the best parts"—said with a grin—"is getting to use bigger brushes." In more serious reflection, he continued: "I find it very freeing, in a sense. In my picture books, I'm always watching to see that the image is appropriate to the story and to the subject matter, and I'm always trying to second-guess what my editor or art director might be looking for. When I do these other things, I do them just for myself. And yet my heart will always be thoroughly grounded in my books for children."[1]

On the following pages a highly selective "gallery tour" gives a glimpse of—as another exhibit at Colby-Sawyer College was aptly titled—*Tomie dePaola's Other Side.*[2]

Figure Study, Pratt Institute
ink and colored pastels on paper
24" x 19 1/4"
circa 1952–1956

Crowd Scene Assignment, Pratt Institute
tempera on illustration board
16" x 19"
circa 1952–1956

Geraniums
oil on canvas
18" x 23 3/4"
1955

Self-portrait
oil on canvas
19" x 29"
1954

Brothers
oil on canvas
18" x 24"
1957

Bobo
oil on canvas
32" x 24"
1966

Cousin Kitty
oil on canvas
16 1/4" x 16 1/4"
1966

Italian Grandparents: Concetta and Antonio
oil on canvas
18" x 24"
1966

FEP
oil on canvas
36" x 36"
1966

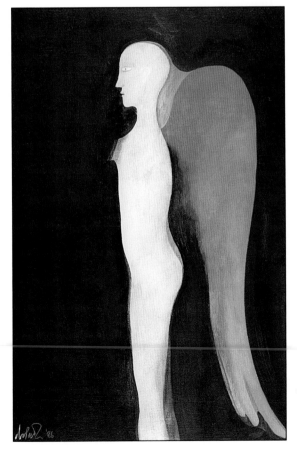

Angel
acrylic on canvas
30" x 20"
1986

155

Satie
acrylic on canvas
20" x 30"
1977

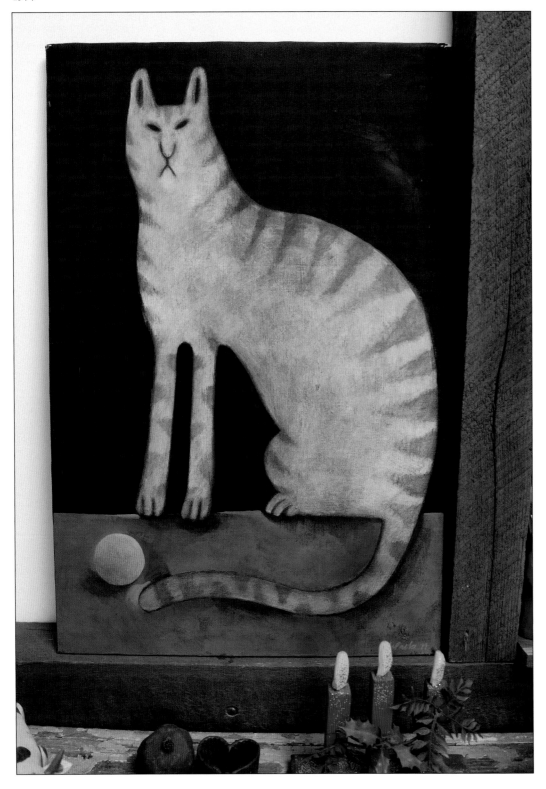

Blue Chair
acrylic on paper
22" x 30"
1989

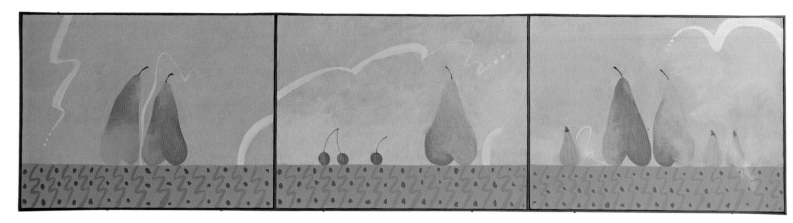

Pears Triptych
acrylic on canvas
72 3/4" x 18 1/4"
1996

Five Gourds
acrylic on wood and on gourds
42 3/4" x 9 3/4" x 11"
1995

Angel on a Pear for Bob—Christmas 1994
acrylic on paper
7 1/2" x 5 1/2"
1994

Watermelon Slice, Pears & Kelly's Horse
acrylic on canvas
18" x 24"
1996

Frida's Table
acrylic on canvas
5' x 4'
1995

161

Dahlias
acrylic on canvas
18" x 24"
1996

Casa Azul (Frida's Blue House)
acrylic on canvas
5' x 4'
2000

What a Peach!
acrylic on canvas
4' x 4'
2000

Pierrot with Five Yellow Birds
acrylic on canvas
3' x 3'
2002

Matisse Madonna
acrylic on canvas
4' x 5'
2009

Red-Haired Madonna
acrylic on canvas
4' x 4'
2007

Red Madonna
acrylic on canvas
3' x 5'
2012

*She Loves Standing in a Newly
Plowed Field in Her New Shoes*
acrylic on canvas
30" x 40"
2013

Tree by Living Water—Psalm 1
acrylic on canvas
24" x 24"
2015

Landscape #17—
Mountains—Creek—
Overflowing
acrylic on canvas
24" x 24"
2015

Landscape #16—Mountains—Creek
acrylic on canvas
24" x 24"
2015

Apples Sixty Years Later
acrylic on canvas
3' x 6'
2014

A Visit from an Old Professor

by Roger Crossgrove, 1999[3]

It was a clear spring day when I visited Tomie recently in his New London home and studio. The flowers and lawns and the views from the gazebo and swimming pool echoed the colors and compositional base that I was familiar with through his picture books. After all, I have been looking at, reading to my children and grandchildren, and collecting his books for more than thirty years.

Inside, I was treated to a visual feast of images—a watercolor of a young man with a lamb on his shoulder, a scene of the Virgin of Guadalupe, an angel on a pear, and a mother and child and a moon. On our way to view slides of his past work (our project for the day), I passed several rows of large acrylic paintings, which I later learned were being photographed and documented for an upcoming exhibition at the Cove Gallery in Wellfleet, Massachusetts. There was a haunting landscape with three trees, a house, and a foreground of fields; a "cherry thief"—a blackbird with a "Who me?" look in his eye and stance; a long bench with a purple-and-green-striped seat cover; and then a huge orange against a blue field, stripped of all nonessentials. I was stopped by the orange, puzzled. It stirred a memory I couldn't quite catch. "Revenge?" The word came and went, surely without connection here.

I spent the afternoon looking at hundreds of images. Tomie (or his mother!) had saved everything—from early childhood drawings through stacks of work from his Pratt Institute days to last week's watercolor of a still life with watermelon. The boxes of Pratt work offer a short, select record of the educational program for training artist-illustrators: figure drawings from Mr. Albert's class, two- and three-dimensional design projects from Mr. Whiteman's class, a pastel and charcoal drawing of Anita Lobel as a Spanish dancer from Mr. Bove's class, a moon juggler, the girls of the Kit Kat Klub with mesh stockings, garters, and hands on hips, a picture of jaunty seductiveness. Here was early evidence of Tomie's inborn ability to see and re-present the telling gesture in line, color, shape, and texture to find just the right image to tell the story.

And then there was the painting of the apples—one of my "Fall Scenes" still-life projects for Sophomore Painting, required of all majors in the illustration program. Tomie's (breakthrough) solution was to make a very big painting some sixty inches long of red apples; it was by far the largest in the class.

When it got to be six thirty that evening, Tomie left Bob (his assistant) and me and went to his "chef's heaven" kitchen to prepare dinner. Later, we joined him—sitting on stools in the kitchen, a glass of Rockford Basket Press Shiraz in hand—while Tomie chopped, stirred, turned, tossed, and tasted. When he announced that dinner was ready, we moved to the dining room, ablaze with candles on the table, on the sideboard, in the candelabra overhead, and in the wall

Summer Lawn, acrylic on canvas, 18" x 24", 1996

Roger Crossgrove and dePaola at author Barbara Elleman's home, 2009.

sconces. More wine for toasting each other's contributions to the slide documentation project at hand and its future, as well as to the dinner—presented picture perfect—and then, of course, to the inevitable good old days when we were at Pratt.

We told stories and interrupted each other with tales about classmates long forgotten as well as those who are now familiar names in libraries, bookstores, museums, galleries, schools, and homes around the world: Susan Jeffers, Chuck Mikolaycak, Arnold and Anita Lobel, John Schoenherr, Gerald McDermott, Cyndy Szekeres—the list went on. Suddenly it was Brooklyn in the 1950s: rows of brownstones, the Myrtle Avenue L, Fort Greene Park, the cannon near the library in the little Pratt Institute park. We talked about the teachers at Pratt and the classmates, the favorites and the ones less so.

As Tomie began telling Bob (had he heard this before?) about his first painting in my sophomore class, I recalled my earlier elusive memory upon seeing that orange, and began to sense that something was about to reveal itself. Tomie set the stage with a grandiose description of the classroom— the easels, stools, and painting tables that had been arranged for each student in semicircles around several shadow boxes, each containing a still life I had set up for that day. He recalled his excitement about his first painting in his first painting class. And what did his shadow box contain? A chunk of black coal and a white hard-cooked egg, beautifully lighted to define the various planes and tonal values as well as the textures and surfaces of the two objects. At least, that's how I saw it. I had been pleased with this exercise in the basics. As for Tomie? I certainly don't remember the classroom mood or any comments made at the time, but it's probably just as well.

Tomie's still-life apples would come later, and his grade would move from the generic C to an A by the end of the term. But that day, I'd given him an egg and a lump of coal. And now on this day, looking at that huge glowing orange, I'd thought "revenge" and, though I didn't ask him, it was—the Revenge of the Egg! Those long years back, a small colorless object had sat motionless and cold against an even colder, more motionless piece of coal. Today, I'd been knocked out by a vibrant orange (egg?) bigger than life, bright, round, ripe, and full. I call that sweet revenge. What a marvelous moment, just one of the many in a long-standing friendship with this wonderful man whose work will be admired and loved for generations to come.

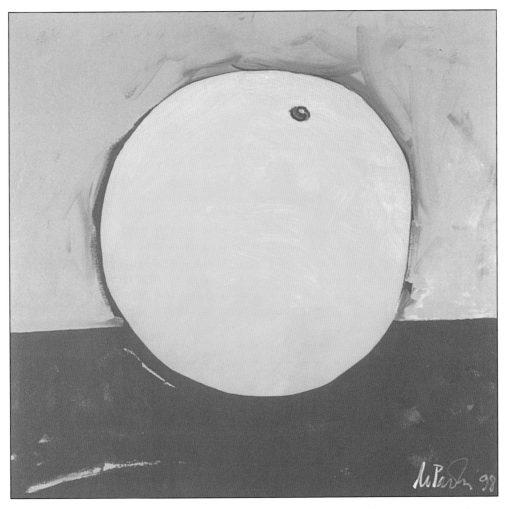

Big Orange, acrylic on canvas, 3' x 3', 1998

The author, Barbara Elleman, in conversation with dePaola at the Eric Carle Museum of Picture Book Art in 2015.

Acknowledgments

My warm appreciation once again to Tomie dePaola and to Bob Hechtel for providing updated information and delightful anecdotes for the new edition of *The Worlds of Tomie dePaola: The Art and Stories of the Legendary Artist and Author* (previously titled *Tomie dePaola: His Art and His Stories*). My thanks to Doug Whiteman for urging me to pursue this revision, for providing me with names and information to start the process moving forward, and for his continuing support; to Emma Ledbetter for her helpful suggestions during the early weeks of writing and revising; and to Kristin Ostby for coming on board midway through this publishing endeavor with always-ready encouragement and wise suggestions. I send appreciation to Alicia Mikles, Amanda Ramirez, and Julia McCarthy for their behind-the-scenes work during at-home directives. And thanks especially to art director Laurent Linn for his splendid creativity and wise understanding in the ways he uses space and color. I also send my appreciation to Alix Kennedy, Rebecca Goggins, Courtney Waring, Ellen Keiter, and Betty Matthews at the Eric Carle Museum of Picture Book Art for their interest and support, and to Sherri Litwack for her ever-ready friendship. And to worldwide appreciators of Tomie's ever-extraordinary work, I echo Trina Schart Hyman's opening tribute—*Viva Tomie!!*

Notes

The dePaola quotations and much of the original information in this book were taken from formal interviews with Tomie dePaola in November 1996 and in May and December 1997, and then were updated in 2020 through casual conversations, telephone calls, and my reviewing notes made during various dePaola visits and interchanges over the intervening years. The statistics on books, mail, and other data were provided by Bob Hechtel.

Chapter 1: A Life

1. *Something about the Author: Autobiography Series*, vol. 15 (Detroit, MI: Gale Research, 1993), 87.
2. *Something about the Author: Autobiography Series*, 15:92.
3. *Southern Vermont Valley News*, October 24, 1980.
4. *Something about the Author: Autobiography Series*, 15:96.
5. Florence Nesci, a friend of the dePaola family, lived in nearby Yalesville, Connecticut.
6. Frances (Franny) McLaughlin-Gill and Kathryn (Fuffy) Abbe were pictured (holding cards number ten and number fifteen) in Guy Trebay's article "All Together Now," which featured top contemporary women photographers in *New York*. *New York*, November 4, 1996, p. 45.
7. Anita Lobel received a 1982 Caldecott Honor for *On Market Street* (Greenwillow), written by Arnold Lobel; Arnold Lobel won the 1981 Caldecott Medal for *Fables* (Harper); John Schoenherr won the 1988 Caldecott Medal for *Owl Moon* (Philomel), written by Jane Yolen; and Ted Lewin received a 1994 Caldecott Honor for *Peppe the Lamplighter* (Lothrop), written by Elisa Bartone.
8. Alice and Martin Provensen wrote and illustrated titles such as *The Year at Maple Hill Farm* (Atheneum), *A Peaceable Kingdom: The Shaker Abecedarius* (Viking), and the Little Golden Book *The Color Kittens*, and were awarded the 1984 Caldecott Medal for *The Glorious Flight: Across the Channel with Louis Blériot* (Viking).
9. Sequence illustration is a technique dePaola often uses to show several events in a sequence of actions with the same characters on the same page. Examples can be found in *"Charlie Needs a Cloak," Mary Had a Little Lamb*, and *The Holy Twins*.
10. French expressionist Georges Rouault (1871–1958) is best known for his mythological and religious canvases.
11. Works by Ben Shahn (1898–1969) hang in the Museum of Modern Art in New York City.
12. The Skowhegan School of Painting and Sculpture is located in Skowhegan, Maine.
13. DePaola quoted Shahn during an interview on *Home Matters*, which aired on the Discovery Channel on October 28 and December 12, 1997.
14. Leo Lionni, *Between Worlds: The Autobiography of Leo Lionni* (New York: Knopf, 1997).
15. Now deceased, Mother Placid resided at the Abbey of Regina Laudis in Bethlehem, Connecticut.
16. The documentary, *The Sinking of the* Andrea Doria, was televised on A&E.
17. DePaola had used "Thomas dePaola" on his traveler's checks to match the signature on his passport.
18. Weston Priory, in Weston, Vermont, is a Benedictine monastery.
19. DePaola married Monique Chéret in 1959; they divorced in 1961.

20. For the Glastonbury Abbey in Hingham, Massachusetts, dePaola designed a crucifix, which was modeled and cast in bronze. He also painted a second crucifix on wood, painted stations of the cross on the chapel walls, painted a mural of Saint Benedict on a chapel wall, lettered the entry-way, and painted three murals in the refectory.

21. The Dominican Retreat and Conference Center, 1945 Union Street, Niskayuna, New York 12309, is the chapel where dePaola created ten-foot-high figures for an expansive mural; it was his first big commission. The mural depicting female saints important to the Dominican order of sisters is the focal point of the chapel. The center's administrator at the time, Jeanne Qualters, said that "teachers familiar with dePaola's books recognize his work when they visit." Karen Bjornland, "Book Signings Planned," *The Daily Gazette* (Schenectady), November 3, 1997.

22. Chronology of dePaola's teaching career:

    1962–1963: instructor of art, Newton College of the Sacred Heart, Newton, Massachusetts

    1963–1966: assistant professor of art, Newton College of the Sacred Heart, Newton, Massachusetts

    1967–1970: assistant professor of art, Lone Mountain College (called San Francisco College of Women before 1969), San Francisco, California

    1972–1973: instructor of art, Chamberlayne Junior College, Boston, Massachusetts

    1973–1976: designer and technical director in speech and theater, Colby-Sawyer College, New London, New Hampshire

    1976–1978: associate professor of art, New England College, Henniker, New Hampshire

    1978–1979: artist-in-residence, New England College, Henniker, New Hampshire

23. Home liturgies were popular in the 1960s among those pulling away from organized religion yet still wanting worship in their lives.

24. "White Bird" was composed in 1967 by David LaFlamme, the leader of the rock group It's a Beautiful Day.

25. Candace Ord Manroe, "Tomie's Christmas Story," *Country Home*, December 1992.

26. Tomie dePaola, "Christmas Is When the Invisible Becomes Visible," Voices of New England, *The Boston Sunday Globe*, December 24, 1995.

27. The Botolph Group, in Cambridge and Boston, Massachusetts, was owned and operated by Celia Hubbard and specialized in contemporary liturgical art.

28. Florence Alexander lived in New York City and was dePaola's artist representative from 1964 until she died in 1993.

29. *Something about the Author: Autobiography Series*, 15:100.

30. The physical science series was called Science Is What and Why. Bernice Kohn Hunt, freelance editor of the series, was also the author of many children's books, including *The Whatchamacallit Book*, illustrated by Tomie dePaola (Putnam, 1996).

31. Andi Axman, "Tomie dePaola's Magical New Hampshire Home," *New Hampshire Home*, November/December 2014, 58–71. Photos by John W. Hession.

Chapter 2: Autobiographical Tales

1. Ellen Roberts, *The Children's Picture Book: How to Write It, How to Sell It* (New York: Writer's Digest, 1981), 20.

2. Tommy (and Tomie) called his paternal grandmother "Nana Fall-River" because she lived in Fall River, Massachusetts. Aunt Nell, a favorite relative of dePaola's, was his mother's aunt.

3. Charles Massey, a New York theatrical manager and a friend of dePaola's, was responsible for hiring new cast members for *A Chorus Line* in its early years on Broadway.

Chapter 3: Strega Nona

1. Strega Nona was conceived on dePaola's doodle pad while he was at a faculty meeting at Colby-Sawyer College in 1974.
2. The Strega Nona doll is produced by MerryMakers, Inc. Strega Nona wall hangings were available from Demco, Inc., in Madison, Wisconsin. Strega Nona pillows and ornaments were by Midwest of Cannon Falls. Strega Nona tote bags were by Kidstamps. The Strega Nona balloon appeared at Universal Studios, Orlando, on September 10, 1996, and at the World Financial Center Children's Book and Activity Fair, in association with Rizzoli Bookstore, on November 12–14, 1993, in New York City.
3. *Strega Nona*, published by Prentice-Hall in 1975, edited by Ellen Roberts, was named an Honor Book by the 1976 Newbery-Caldecott committee, chaired by Harriet B. Quimby. The medal that year was awarded to Leo and Diane Dillon for *Why Mosquitoes Buzz in People's Ears* (Dial).
4. Grandma Concetta, Strega Nona's grandmother, is the name of dePaola's real Italian grandmother. She is Nana Fall-River in *The Baby Sister* and Grandmother in *Watch Out for the Chicken Feet in Your Soup*.
5. Bette Peltola's remarks appear in *Tomie dePaola: A Portfolio*, prepared by the 1990 United States Board on Books for Young People's Andersen committee and G. P. Putnam's Sons for presentation to the International Board on Books for Young People's Hans Christian Andersen international jury.

Chapter 4: Folktales

1. Piero Canuto was owner-chef of La Meridiana Restaurant in Wilmot Flat, New Hampshire. DePaola, unsuccessful in his search to find a written version of the legend, concluded that it was a bit of oral lore; Canuto confirmed that by saying he remembered hearing the legend as a child from his teacher.
2. Margaret Looper, a reading consultant in Huntsville, Texas, urged dePaola to tell and illustrate the tale about the Texas bluebonnet and sent him background information on the Comanche people.

Chapter 5: Religious and Spiritual Themes

1. Pura Belpré, a well-known storyteller, was honored in 1996 by the creation of an award in her name. Administered by the American Library Association and REFORMA, the award honors Latino/Latina writers and illustrators whose work best portrays, affirms, and celebrates the Latino/Latina cultural experience in the work of literature for youths.
2. F. R. Webber, *Church Symbolism: An Explanation of the More Important Symbols of the Old and New Testament, the Primitive, the Mediaeval and the Modern Church*, 2nd ed. (Cleveland: J. H. Hansen, 1938), 39.
3. Saint Francis was born in 1182; his eight hundredth birth anniversary inspired numerous celebrations around the world.
4. Giotto di Bondone (1267–1337), *St. Francis Preaching to the Birds*, Upper Basilica of San Francesco, Assisi, Italy.
5. Vittore Carpaccio (1450–1525/26), *The Miracle of the Relic of the True Cross on the Rialto Bridge*, Galleria dell'Accademia, Venice, Italy.

Chapter 6: Christmas Stories

1. Patricia Bunning Stevens, *Merry Christmas: A History of the Holiday* (New York: Macmillan, 1979).

Chapter 7: Mother Goose and Other Collections

1. Constance Congdon, playwright, poet, and children's book author, is a professor at Amherst College, Amherst, Massachusetts.
2. The Illustrators' Exhibition is held annually at the Children's Book Fair, Bologna, Italy.
3. Joy Backhouse, then the children's editor at Methuen Children's Books Ltd., was dePaola's London editor; *Tomie dePaola's Mother Goose* was published in England in 1985.
4. Nanette Stevenson was art director at Putnam from July 1981 to February 1994.
5. Iona and Peter Opie, *The Oxford Nursery Rhyme Book* (New York: Oxford University Press, 1955), preface.
6. The early version dePaola remembered is probably *The Real Mother Goose*, illustrated by Blanche Fisher Wright (Macmillan/Checkerboard, 1916).

Chapter 8: Informational Books

1. The quote couldn't be located, and dePaola did not remember its source. As a first-time illustrator, however, he keenly felt the words; later, in retrospect, he found them "highly complimentary."
2. The Kerlan Collection at the University of Minnesota holds most of dePaola's early manuscripts and artwork up to the mid-1970s as well as some later work.
3. Information from Holiday House publicity files.

Chapter 9: Story Making: Patterns, Visual Themes, and Motifs

1. Pablo Picasso (1881–1973), *The Old Guitarist*, the Art Institute of Chicago.
2. Henri Matisse and Pablo Picasso were friends, but history also attests to their frequent quarrels about art—noted in Patrick O'Brian's *Picasso: A Biography* (Putnam, 1976).
3. Claude Monet, Josephine Baker, Isadora Duncan, Zelda Fitzgerald, and Ernest Hemingway are a few of the characters appearing at Gertrude (Stein) and Alice's (B. Toklas) salon.
4. Georges Braque (1882–1963), *Still Life with Score by Satie*, the Centre Pompidou, Paris. DePaola's cat Satie was named after the composer Erik Satie. When dePaola was driving to the airport in Manchester, New Hampshire, to pick up his cat, which was being shipped from New York, music by Satie was playing on the car radio. This motivated dePaola to call the cat "Satie."
5. Examples include Jacqueline Davies and Melissa Sweet's *The Boy Who Drew Birds: A Story of John James Audubon* (HMH Books for Young Readers, 2004), Marjorie Blain Parker and Holly Berry's *Colorful Dreamer: The Story of Artist Henri Matisse* (Dial Books for Young Readers, 2012), and Robert Burleigh and Wendell Minor's *Edward Hopper Paints His World* (Henry Holt and Co., 2014).
6. Corita Kent, also known as Sister Corita, was part of a contemporary liturgical art movement in the late 1950s and early 1960s. After she left the convent, she signed her work "Corita."

7. Sketches and accompanying notes for *Big Anthony and the Magic Ring* (now called *Strega Nona's Magic Ring*) are at the Kerlan Collection, University of Minnesota, Minneapolis. Jean-François Millet (1814–1875), *The Angelus*, Musée d'Orsay, Paris.

8. Pieter Brueghel, the Elder (1525/30–1569), *Children's Games*, Kunsthistorisches Museum, Vienna; the Bayeux Tapestry, Centre Guillaume le Conquérant, Bayeux, France.

9. Tamas Hofer and Edit Fel, *Hungarian Folk Art* (New York: Oxford University Press, 1979).

Chapter 10: Publishing History

1. Blanche Gregory, of Blanche C. Gregory, Inc., represented adult authors such as Joyce Carol Oates.

2. The Agents' Guild was an organization for people who represented authors and artists in publishing.

3. Bernice Kohn Hunt was the editor of *Sound*, dePaola's first book; Lisa Miller was the author.

4. Russell Freedman, *Holiday House: The First Fifty Years* (New York: Holiday House, 1985).

5. *The Quicksand Book* quote was from an unnamed reviewer in the Los Angeles school system. David Macaulay is the author of *Cathedral*, *City*, *Pyramid*, and the Caldecott Medal Book *Black and White*, published by Houghton Mifflin.

6. In the preseparation process the artist separates the colors by preparing a key plate and one or more overlays. Each color requires a separate overlay; when printed, they form a multicolor picture.

7. Whitebird Books:

The Little Snowgirl: An Old Russian Tale, adapted and illustrated by Carolyn Croll, 1989

Tony's Bread: An Italian Folktale, written and illustrated by Tomie dePaola, 1989

The Badger and the Magic Fan: A Japanese Folktale, adapted by Tony Johnston, illustrated by Tomie dePaola, 1990

Good Morning, Granny Rose: An Arkansas Folktale, retold and illustrated by Warren Ludwig, 1990

Quail Song: A Pueblo Indian Tale, adapted by Valerie Scho Carey, illustrated by Ivan Barnett, 1990

The Stonecutter: An Indian Folktale, retold and illustrated by Pam Newton, 1990

Old Noah's Elephants: An Israeli Folktale, adapted and illustrated by Warren Ludwig, 1991

The Three Brothers: A German Folktale, adapted and illustrated by Carolyn Croll, 1991

Chancay and the Secret of Fire: A Peruvian Folktale, written and illustrated by Donald Charles, 1992

The Green Gourd: A North Carolina Folktale, retold by C. W. Hunter, illustrated by Tony Griego, 1992

Jamie O'Rourke and the Big Potato: An Irish Folktale, retold and illustrated by Tomie dePaola, 1992

The Singing Fir Tree: A Swiss Folktale, retold by Marti Stone, illustrated by Barry Root, 1992

The Legend of the Persian Carpet, retold by Tomie dePaola, illustrated by Claire Ewart, 1993

Magic Spring: A Korean Folktale, retold and illustrated by Nami Rhee, 1993

The Rooster Who Went to His Uncle's Wedding: A Latin American Folktale, retold by Alma Flor Ada, illustrated by Kathleen Kuchera, 1993

Under the Midsummer Sky: A Swedish Folktale, written by Carole Lexa Schaefer, illustrated by Pat Geddes, 1994

8. Former CEO of Penguin Putnam Phyllis Grann wrote a board book called *I Will Talk to You, Little One*, with artwork by dePaola. Grann custom-published the book with Simon & Schuster's Little Simon imprint, and donated more than two hundred thousand copies to City's First Readers, for distribution as a gift to families of newborns across New York City.

Chapter 12: DePaola's Non-Book Art

1. Deborah McKew, "Talking with Tomie dePaola," *Upper Valley Magazine*, November/December 1992.

2. *Tomie dePaola's Other Side* was an exhibit at Colby-Sawyer College in 1991.

3. Roger Crossgrove (1921–2016), a lifelong friend, was one of dePaola's early painting teachers, and he attended the opening of the Eric Carle Museum's exhibition of dePaola's work in 2009, which was curated by Barbara Elleman. He taught at Pratt Institute for fifteen years before becoming head of the art department at the University of Connecticut, where he was later named professor emeritus. When Crossgrove celebrated his eightieth birthday, dePaola gave a tribute in honor of his onetime teacher, then mentor, and longtime friend. When Crossgrove passed away in 2016, dePaola was one of the speakers at his memorial service.

Major Awards, Events, and Recognitions

1958. Exhibits at first group show (non-book art), Southern Vermont Arts Center, Manchester, Vermont

1961. Exhibits at first one-man show (non-book art), the Botolph Group, Boston

1965. Illustrates first book, *Sound*, by Lisa Miller, Coward-McCann

1966. Writes and illustrates *The Wonderful Dragon of Timlin*, Bobbs-Merrill

1968. Receives Award of Excellence, Art Directors' Club of Boston

1969. Receives Silver Award, Franklin Prize Competition, Franklin Typographers, New York

1970. Exhibits *The Journey of the Kiss* artwork in the American Institute of Graphic Arts of Outstanding Children's Books

1972. Publishes first full-color book, *The Wind and the Sun*, Ginn

1974. Receives first Notable Children's Book citation for *"Charlie Needs a Cloak"* from the American Library Association (Association for Library Service to Children)

1976. Receives Caldecott Honor Book award for *Strega Nona*

1977. Receives second place, Japan's Owl Prize, for *Strega Nona*

1977. Exhibits at *Twelfth Exhibition of Original Pictures of International Children's Picture Books*, sponsored by Maruzen Co., Ltd., and Shiko-Sha Co., Ltd., Japan

1978. Exhibits at Illustrators' Exhibition, Children's Book Fair, Bologna, Italy

1978. Receives the Nakamori Prize, Japan, for *Strega Nona*

1978. Receives the American Institute of Graphic Arts Award for *Helga's Dowry*

1978. Exhibits *The Clown of God* and *Pancakes for Breakfast* at the Twenty-Ninth International Exhibition of Children's and Youth Books, International Youth Library, Munich, Germany

1979. *Bill and Pete, The Clown of God, Four Scary Stories, Jamie's Tiger, Pancakes for Breakfast*, and *The Popcorn Book* are selected for Children's Choices, International Reading Association (now the International Literacy Association) and the Children's Book Council

1980. Exhibits at the first *The Original Art* exhibition, Master Eagle Gallery, New York, New York

1980. Wins the Garden State Children's Book Award for younger nonfiction from the New Jersey Library Association for *The Quicksand Book*

1980. Appointed to the board of advisors, Society of Children's Book Writers and Illustrators

1981. Opens *The Clown of God* at the Children's Theatre Company in Minneapolis

1981. Receives Kerlan Award for "singular attainment in children's literature," University of Minnesota, Minneapolis

1982. Exhibits at *A Decade of the Original Art of the Best Illustrated Children's Books, 1970–1980*, University of Connecticut Library, Storrs, Connecticut

1982. Receives a Boston Globe–Horn Book Honor award for *The Friendly Beasts*

1982. Designs Christmas catalog cover and shopping bag for Neiman Marcus department stores

1982. Receives Golden Kite Award for Illustration, Society of Children's Book Writers and Illustrators, for *Giorgio's Village*

1983. Receives Critici in Erba commendation from the Bologna Biennale for *The Friendly Beasts* at the Children's Book Fair, Bologna, Italy

1983. Receives Regina Medal, Catholic Library Association, "in recognition of outstanding accomplishments in the field of children's literature"

1983. Exhibits at Twenty-Fifth Annual Exhibition, Society of Illustrators, New York, New York

1983. Designs Children's Book Week poster "Get into Books" for the Children's Book Council

1983. Designs first of several popcorn cans for the Popcorn Factory

1985. Exhibits artwork for *Tattie's River Journey*, by Shirley Rousseau Murphy, at the Biennial of Illustrations, Bratislava, Slovakia

1985. Receives doctor of letters, *honoris causa*, Colby-Sawyer College, New London, New Hampshire

1986. Signs global agreement with Putnam

1986. Receives David McCord Children's Literature Citation, first recipient, for "significant contribution to excellence in books for children," sponsored by Framingham State College and the Nobscot Reading Council of the International Reading Association (now the International Literacy Association), Framingham, Massachusetts

1987. Exhibits books and non-book art in *Tomie dePaola: A Retrospective* at Nashua Arts and Science Center, Nashua, New Hampshire

1987. Receives Golden Kite Honor for Illustration, Society of Children's Book Writers and Illustrators, for Carolyn Craven's *What the Mailman Brought*

1990. Named US nominee for the Hans Christian Andersen Award in Illustration given by the International Board on Books for Young People

1990. Receives James Smithson Bicentennial Medal, Smithsonian Institution

1990. Opens *Tomie dePaola's Mother Goose* at the Children's Theatre Company in Minneapolis

1991. Opens a non-book art show at Cove Gallery, Wellfleet, Massachusetts, and *Tomie dePaola's Other Side* at Sawyer Center, Colby-Sawyer College, New London, New Hampshire

1991. Dedicates the Tomie dePaola Room, Tracy Memorial Library, New London, New Hampshire

1992. Opens the new Thoresen Gallery in the Kraft Education Center in the Art Institute of Chicago, with a one-man show

1993. Receives Helen Keating Ott Award, Church and Synagogue Library Association

1993. Creates an annual art scholarship in his hometown of Meriden, Connecticut

1993. Appears on *Barney and Friends*, the first children's illustrator to be on the program

1994. Receives doctor of humane letters, *honoris causa*, Saint Anselm College, Manchester, New Hampshire

1995. Exhibits *Tomie Turns 60!* at Cedar Rapids Museum of Art, Cedar Rapids, Iowa

1995. Issues Midwest of Cannon Fall's Tomie dePaola Giftware line

1995. Presents to First Lady Hillary Clinton an autographed copy of numbered, limited-edition poster created for Food Research and Action Center

1996. Receives doctor of humane letters, *honoris causa*, Notre Dame College, Manchester, New Hampshire

1996. Receives Milner Award, Atlanta-Fulton Public Library System, Atlanta, Georgia

1997. Is a guest at the White House for an event honoring the Reading Is Fundamental national poster contest winner and the National RIF Reader

1997. Named a Literary Light, Associates of the Boston Public Library, Boston, Massachusetts

1998. Receives the Keene State College Children's Literature Festival Award, Keene, New Hampshire

1998. Begins publishing serigraphs with the Beacon Fine Arts Gallery, Red Bank, New Jersey

1998. Presents keynote speech, Children's Book Council of Australia, Fourth National Conference

1999. Publishes first chapter book, *26 Fairmount Avenue* (Putnam)

1999. Bestows upon the Northeast Children's Literature Collection at the Thomas J. Dodd Research Center at the University of Connecticut his backlist manuscripts and art, which are celebrated with a two-day festival

1999. *Strega Nona* and *The Art Lesson* are among the one hundred books selected for Read Across America, a National Education Association initiative to promote reading among children

1999. Receives doctor of fine arts, *honoris causa*, University of Connecticut, Storrs, Connecticut

1999. Selected as one of "100 People Who Shaped the Century" in New Hampshire by *Concord Monitor*

1999. Receives doctor of humane letters, honoris causa, Emerson College, Boston, Massachusetts

1999. Receives Living Treasure Award, New Hampshire Governor's Arts Awards

1999. Subject of Barbara Elleman's *Tomie dePaola: His Art and His Stories*, Putnam

2000. Receives Newbery Honor Book award for *26 Fairmount Avenue*

2000. Receives I Migliori Award, the Pirandello Lyceum Institute of Italian-American Studies, Research and Cultural Dissemination, East Boston, Massachusetts

2000. Receives Town Award, Colby-Sawyer College, New London, New Hampshire

2000. Receives Jeremiah Ludington Memorial Award, Educational Paperback Association

2001. Receives Granite State Award, Plymouth State College, Plymouth, New Hampshire

2002. Receives doctor of humane letters, *honoris causa*, Georgetown University, Washington, DC

2003. Receives doctor of letters, *honoris causa*, New England College, Henniker, New Hampshire

2003. Receives Jo Osborne Award for Humor in Children's Literature, the Ohio Library Foundation

2003. Receives Lifetime Achievement Award, New Hampshire Writers' Project

2007. Receives Sarah Josepha Hale Award, Richards Free Library, Newport, New Hampshire

2007. Receives Distinguished Service Award, Northeast Children's Literature Collection, University of Connecticut, Storrs, Connecticut

2008. Receives New England Book Award, New England Independent Booksellers Association

2009. Receives honorary doctoral degree, Pratt Institute, Brooklyn, New York

2009. Exhibits *Drawings from the Heart: Tomie dePaola Turns 75*, curated by Barbara Elleman, at Eric Carle Museum of Picture Book Art, Amherst, Massachusetts

2011. Receives Children's Literature Legacy Award (previously called the Laura Ingalls Wilder Award) for "substantial and lasting contribution to literature for children"

2012. Receives Lifetime Achievement Award, Society of Illustrators, the Original Art show, New York, New York

2012. Work named to the Top 125 Pratt Icons of All Time, Pratt Institute, Brooklyn, New York

2018. Receives doctor of fine arts, *honoris causa*, New Hampshire Institute of Art, Manchester, New Hampshire

Bibliography

Titles Written (or Edited) and Illustrated by Tomie dePaola

Adelita: A Mexican Cinderella Story, Putnam, 2002

Andy & Sandy and the Big Talent Show, with Jim Lewis, Simon & Schuster Books for Young Readers, 2017

Andy & Sandy and the First Snow, with Jim Lewis, Simon & Schuster Books for Young Readers, 2016

Andy & Sandy's Anything Adventure, with Jim Lewis, Simon & Schuster Books for Young Readers, 2016

Andy, That's My Name, Prentice-Hall, 1973; reissued, Simon & Schuster Books for Young Readers, 2015

Angels, Angels Everywhere, Putnam, 2005

The Art Lesson, Putnam, 1989

Baby's First Christmas, Putnam, 1988

The Baby Sister, Putnam, 1996

Big Anthony and the Magic Ring—see *Strega Nona's Magic Ring*

Big Anthony, His Story, Putnam, 1998

Bill and Pete, Putnam, 1978

Bill and Pete Go Down the Nile, Putnam, 1987

Bill and Pete to the Rescue, Putnam, 1998

The Birds of Bethlehem, Putnam, 2012

Bonjour, Mr. Satie, Putnam, 1991

Boss for a Day, Grosset & Dunlap, 2001

Brava, Strega Nona! A Heartwarming Pop-Up Book, Putnam, 2008

The Bubble Factory, Grosset & Dunlap, 1996

The Cat on the Dovrefell: A Christmas Tale, Putnam, 1979

"Charlie Needs a Cloak," Prentice-Hall, 1973

The Christmas Pageant, Winston Press, 1978

Christmas Remembered, Putnam, 2006

Christopher, the Holy Giant, Holiday House, 1994

The Cloud Book, Holiday House, 1975

The Clown of God, Harcourt Brace Jovanovich, 1978; reissued, Simon & Schuster Books for Young Readers, 2018

The Comic Adventures of Old Mother Hubbard and Her Dog, Harcourt Brace Jovanovich, 1981; reissued, Simon & Schuster Books for Young Readers, 2020

Country Angel Christmas, Putnam, 1995

David and Goliath, Winston Press, 1984

Days of the Blackbird: A Tale of Northern Italy, Putnam, 1997

An Early American Christmas, Holiday House, 1987

The Family Christmas Tree Book, Holiday House, 1980

Fight the Night, Lippincott, 1968; reissued, Simon & Schuster Books for Young Readers, 2020

Fin M'Coul: The Giant of Knockmany Hill, Holiday House, 1981

The First Christmas: A Pop-Up Book, Putnam, 1984

Flicks, Harcourt Brace Jovanovich, 1979

For the Duration, Putnam, 2009

Four Stories for Four Seasons, Prentice-Hall, 1977

Francis, the Poor Man of Assisi, Holiday House, 1982

The Friendly Beasts: An Old English Christmas Carol, Putnam, 1981

Get Dressed, Santa!, Grosset & Dunlap, 1996

Giorgio's Village: A Pop-Up Book, Putnam, 1982

Guess Who's Coming to Santa's for Dinner?, Putnam, 2004; reissued, Simon & Schuster Books for Young Readers, 2020

Haircuts for Little Lambs (originally titled *Haircuts for the Woolseys*), Putnam, 1998; reissued, Little Simon, 2000

Helga's Dowry: A Troll Love Story, Harcourt Brace Jovanovich, 1977

Here We All Are, Putnam, 2000

Hide-and-Seek All Week, Grosset & Dunlap, 2001

The Hunter and the Animals: A Wordless Picture Book, Holiday House, 1981

I'm Still Scared, Putnam, 2006

Jack, Penguin, 2014

Jamie O'Rourke and the Big Potato: An Irish Folktale, Putnam/Whitebird, 1992

Jamie O'Rourke and the Pooka, Putnam, 2000

Jingle the Christmas Clown, Putnam, 1992

Joe and the Snow, Hawthorn, 1968

The Journey of the Kiss, Hawthorn, 1970

The Kids' Cat Book, Holiday House, 1979

Kit and Kat, Grosset & Dunlap, 1994

The Knight and the Dragon, Putnam, 1980

The Lady of Guadalupe, Holiday House, 1980

The Legend of Old Befana: An Italian Christmas Story, Harcourt Brace Jovanovich, 1980; reissued, Simon & Schuster Books for Young Readers, 2017

The Legend of the Bluebonnet: An Old Tale of Texas, Putnam, 1983

The Legend of the Indian Paintbrush, Putnam, 1988

The Legend of the Poinsettia, Putnam, 1994

Let the Whole Earth Sing Praise, Putnam, 2011

Little Grunt and the Big Egg: A Prehistoric Fairy Tale, Holiday House, 1990; reissued, Putnam, 2006

Look and Be Grateful, Holiday House, 2015

The Magical World of Strega Nona: A Treasury, Penguin, 2015

Marcos Colors: Red, Yellow, Blue, Putnam, 2003

Marcos Counts: One, Two, Three, Putnam, 2003

Marianna May and Nursey, Holiday House, 1983; reissued, Simon & Schuster Books for Young Readers, 2020

Mary, the Mother of Jesus, Holiday House, 1995

Meet the Barkers: Morgan and Moffat Go to School, Grosset & Dunlap, 2001

Merry Christmas, Strega Nona, Harcourt Brace Jovanovich, 1986

Michael Bird-Boy, Prentice-Hall, 1975; reissued, Simon & Schuster Books for Young Readers, 2015

The Miracles of Jesus, Holiday House, 1987

The Monsters' Ball, Hawthorn, 1970

My First Angels, Grosset & Dunlap, 2011

My First Bible Stories, Grosset & Dunlap, 2010

My First Chanukah, Putnam, 1989

My First Christmas, Grosset & Dunlap, 2015

My First Christmas Carols, Grosset & Dunlap, 2010

My First Easter, Putnam, 1990

My First Fairy Tales, Grosset & Dunlap, 2009

My First Halloween, Putnam, 1991

My First Legends: The Story of Bluebonnet, Grosset & Dunlap, 2011

My First Mother Goose, Grosset & Dunlap, 2009

My First Passover, Putnam, 1990

My First Songs, Grosset & Dunlap, 2010

My First Thanksgiving, Putnam, 1992

My Mother Is So Smart!, Putnam, 2010

The Mysterious Giant of Barletta, Harcourt Brace Jovanovich, 1984

Nana Upstairs & Nana Downstairs, Putnam, 1973; reissued, Putnam, 1998

A New Barker in the House, Grosset & Dunlap, 2002

The Night of Las Posadas, Putnam, 1999

Noah and the Ark, Winston, 1983

Now One Foot, Now the Other, Putnam, 1981; reissued 2005

Oliver Button Is a Sissy, Harcourt Brace Jovanovich, 1979; reissued, Simon & Schuster Books for Young Readers, 2017

On My Way, Putnam, 2001

Pancakes for Breakfast, Harcourt Brace Jovanovich, 1978

The Parables of Jesus, Holiday House, 1987; reissued as *The Good Samaritan and Other Parables*, Holiday House, 2017

Parker Pig, Esquire, Hawthorn, 1969

Pascual and the Kitchen Angels, Putnam, 2004

Patrick, Patron Saint of Ireland, Holiday House, 1992

The Popcorn Book, Holiday House, 1978; reissued, Holiday House, 2018

The Prince of the Dolomites: An Old Italian Tale, Harcourt Brace Jovanovich, 1980

Queen Esther, Harper & Row, 1986

The Quicksand Book, Holiday House, 1977

Quiet, Simon & Schuster Books for Young Readers, 2018

Sing, Pierrot, Sing: A Picture Book in Mime, Harcourt Brace Jovanovich, 1983

The Song of Francis, Putnam, 2009

Songs of the Fog Maiden, Holiday House, 1979

The Story of the Three Wise Kings, Putnam, 1983; reissued, Simon & Schuster Books for Young Readers, 2020

Strega Nona and Her Tomatoes, Simon & Schuster/Simon Spotlight, 2017

Strega Nona and the Twins, Simon & Schuster/Simon Spotlight, 2017

Strega Nona: An Original Tale, Prentice-Hall, 1975; reissued, Simon & Schuster Books for Young Readers, 2015

Strega Nona Does It Again, Putnam, 2013

Strega Nona, Her Story, Putnam, 1996

Strega Nona Meets Her Match, Putnam, 1993

Strega Nona's Gift, Putnam, 2011

Strega Nona's Harvest, Putnam, 2009

Strega Nona's Magic Lessons, Harcourt Brace Jovanovich, 1982; reissued, Simon & Schuster Books for Young Readers, 2017

Strega Nona's Magic Ring (originally titled *Big Anthony and the Magic Ring*), Harcourt Brace Jovanovich, 1979; reissued, Simon & Schuster Books for Young Readers, 2018

Strega Nona Takes a Vacation, Putnam, 2000

Things to Make and Do for Valentine's Day, Franklin Watts, 1976

Things Will Never Be the Same, Putnam, 2003

The Three Friends and the Apples, Scholastic, 2000

The Three Friends and the Leaves, Scholastic, 2000

The Three Friends and the Pumpkins, Scholastic, 2000

The Three Friends Go to School, Scholastic, 2000

Tom, Putnam, 1993

Tomie dePaola's Book of Bible Stories, Putnam/Zondervan, 1990

Tomie dePaola's Book of Christmas Carols, Putnam, 1987

Tomie dePaola's Book of Poems, Putnam, 1988

Tomie dePaola's Book of the Old Testament (Old Testament text with illustrations, from *Tomie dePaola's Book of Bible Stories*), Putnam, 1995

Tomie dePaola's Country Farm, Putnam, 1984

Tomie dePaola's Favorite Nursery Tales, Putnam, 1986

Tomie dePaola's Front Porch Tales & North Country Whoppers, Putnam, 2007

Tomie dePaola's Kitten Kids (*Katie, Kit, and Cousin Tom*; *Pajamas for Kit*; *Katie and Kit at the Beach*; *Katie's Good Idea*), Simon & Schuster, 1986

Tomie dePaola's Make Your Own Christmas Cards, Price Stern Sloan, 1998

Tomie dePaola's Mother Goose, Putnam, 1985

Tomie dePaola's Mother Goose Story Streamers, Putnam, 1984

Tomie's Little Mother Goose, Putnam, 1997

Tony's Bread: An Italian Folktale, Putnam/Whitebird, 1989

Too Many Bunnies (originally titled *Too Many Hopkins*), Putnam, 1989; reissued, Little Simon, 2000

Trouble in the Barkers' Class, Grosset & Dunlap, 2003

26 Fairmount Avenue, Putnam, 1999

The Unicorn and the Moon, Ginn, 1973

Watch Out for the Chicken Feet in Your Soup, Prentice-Hall, 1974

What a Year, Putnam, 2002

When Andy Met Sandy, Simon & Schuster Books for Young Readers, 2016

When Everyone Was Fast Asleep, Holiday House, 1976

Why?, Putnam, 2007

The Wind and the Sun, Ginn, 1972

The Wonderful Dragon of Timlin, Bobbs-Merrill, 1966

Titles Illustrated by Tomie dePaola (Unless Otherwise Noted)

Adler, David A. *The Carsick Zebra and Other Animal Riddles*. Holiday House, 1983.

Alexander, Sue. *Marc the Magnificent*. Pantheon, 1978.

Alexenberg, Melvin L. *Light and Sight*. Prentice-Hall, 1969.

Alexenberg, Melvin L. *Sound Science*. Prentice-Hall, 1968.

Andersen, Hans Christian. *The Emperor's New Clothes: An All-Star Illustrated Retelling of the Classic Fairy Tale*, illustrated by Tomie dePaola et al. Harcourt Brace, 1998.

Baker, Sanna Anderson. *Who's a Friend of the Water-Spurting Whale*. David C. Cook, 1987.

Balestrino, Philip. *Hot As an Ice Cube*. Crowell, 1971.

Belpré, Pura, reteller. *The Tiger and the Rabbit, and Other Tales*. Lippincott, 1965.

Bennett, Jill. *Teeny Tiny*. Putnam, 1986.

Bly, Robert. *The Morning Glory*. Kayak Books, 1969.

Boylan, Eleanor. *How to Be a Puppeteer*. McCall Publishing, 1970.

Calhoun, Mary. *Old Man Whickutt's Donkey*. Parents' Magazine Press, 1975.

Coerr, Eleanor. *The Mixed-Up Mystery Smell*. Putnam, 1976.

Cohen, Peter Zachary. *Authorized Autumn Charts of the Upper Red Canoe River Country*. Atheneum, 1972.

Cole, William, selector. *Oh, Such Foolishness!* Lippincott, 1978.

Craven, Carolyn. *What the Mailman Brought*. Putnam, 1987.

Davies, Valentine. *Miracle on 34th Street*. Harcourt Brace Jovanovich, 1984.

Durrell, Ann, Jean Craighead George, and Katherine Paterson, eds. *The Big Book for Our Planet*, written and illustrated by Tomie dePaola et al. Dutton, 1993.

Eichner, James A. *The Cabinet of the President of the United States*. Franklin Watts, 1968.

Emrich, Duncan, ed. *The Folklore of Love and Courtship*. American Heritage Press, 1970.

Emrich, Duncan, ed. *The Folklore of Weddings and Marriage*. American Heritage Press, 1970.

Epstein, Sam and Beryl. *Hold Everything*. Holiday House, 1973.

Epstein, Sam and Beryl. *Look in the Mirror*. Holiday House, 1973.

Epstein, Sam and Beryl. *Pick It Up*. Holiday House, 1971.

Epstein, Sam and Beryl. *Take This Hammer*. Hawthorn, 1969.

Epstein, Sam and Beryl. *Who Needs Holes?* Hawthorn, 1970.

Ernst, Kathryn F. *Danny and His Thumb*. Prentice-Hall, 1973.

Farber, Norma. *Six Impossible Things Before Breakfast*, illustrated by Tomie dePaola et al. Addison-Wesley, 1977.

Farber, Norma. *This Is the Ambulance Leaving the Zoo*. Dutton, 1975.

Fisher, John. *John Fisher's Magic Book*. Prentice-Hall, 1971.

For Our Children: A Book to Benefit the Pediatric AIDS Foundation, illustrated by Tomie dePaola et al. Disney Press, 1991.

Frith, Margaret. *Frida Kahlo: The Artist Who Painted Herself*. Grosset & Dunlap, 2003.

Fritz, Jean. *Can't You Make Them Behave, King George?* Coward-McCann, 1977.

Fritz, Jean. *The Good Giants and the Bad Pukwudgies*. Putnam, 1982.

Fritz, Jean. *The Great Adventure of Christopher Columbus: A Pop-Up Book*. Putnam/Grosset, 1992.

Fritz, Jean. *Shh! We're Writing the Constitution*. Putnam, 1987.

Gauch, Patricia Lee. *The Little Friar Who Flew*. Putnam, 1980.

Gauch, Patricia Lee. *Once upon a Dinkelsbühl*. Putnam, 1977.

Graham, John. *I Love You, Mouse*. Harcourt Brace Jovanovich, 1976; re-released with full-color illustrations, Putnam, 2008.

Grann, Phyllis E. *I Will Talk to You, Little One*. Simon & Schuster/Little Simon, 2017.

Hale, Sarah Josepha. *Mary Had a Little Lamb*. Holiday House, 1984.

Hall, Malcolm. *Edward, Benjamin & Butter*. Coward-McCann, 1981.

Hancock, Sibyl. *Mario's Mystery Machine*. Putnam, 1972.

Hardendorff, Jeanne B., selector. *Tricky Peik and Other Picture Tales*. Lippincott, 1967.

Hopkins, Lee Bennett, selector. *Beat the Drum: Independence Day Has Come*. Harcourt Brace Jovanovich, 1977.

Hopkins, Lee Bennett, selector. *Easter Buds Are Springing: Poems for Easter*. Harcourt Brace Jovanovich, 1979.

Hopkins, Lee Bennett, selector. *Good Morning to You, Valentine: Poems for Valentine's Day*. Harcourt Brace Jovanovich, 1976.

Houselander, Caryll. *Petook: An Easter Story*. Holiday House, 1988.

Hunt, Bernice Kohn. *The Whatchamacallit Book*. Putnam, 1976.

Jacobs, Leland Blair, selector. *Poetry for Chuckles and Grins*. Garrard, 1968.

Jane, Mary C. *The Rocking-Chair Ghost*. Lippincott, 1969.

Jennings, Michael. *Robin Goodfellow and the Giant Dwarf*. McGraw-Hill, 1981.

Johnston, Tony. *Alice Nizzy Nazzy: The Witch of Santa Fe*. Putnam, 1995.

Johnston, Tony. *The Badger and the Magic Fan*. Putnam/Whitebird, 1990.

Johnston, Tony. *Four Scary Stories*. Putnam, 1978.

Johnston, Tony. *Odd Jobs*. Putnam, 1977.

Johnston, Tony. *Odd Jobs and Friends*. Putnam, 1982.

Johnston, Tony. *Pages of Music*. Putnam, 1988.

Johnston, Tony. *The Quilt Story*. Putnam, 1985.

Johnston, Tony. *The Tale of Rabbit and Coyote*. Putnam, 1994.

Johnston, Tony. *The Vanishing Pumpkin*. Putnam, 1983.

Keller, Charles, and Richard Baker, compilers. *The Star-Spangled Banana and Other Revolutionary Riddles*. Prentice-Hall, 1974.

Klein, Cheryl B. *Wings*. Simon & Schuster/Atheneum Books for Young Readers, 2019.

Kroll, Steven. *Fat Magic*. Holiday House, 1978.

Kroll, Steven. *Santa's Crash-Bang Christmas*. Holiday House, 1977.

Kroll, Steven. *The Tyrannosaurus Game*. Holiday House, 1976.

Larrick, Nancy, and Wendy Lamb, eds. *To Ride a Butterfly*, written and illustrated by Tomie dePaola et al. Bantam Doubleday Dell, 1991.

Lewis, Naomi, reteller. *The Flying Trunk and Other Stories from Hans Andersen*, illustrated by Tomie dePaola et al. Andersen Press, 1986.

Lexau, Joan M. *Finders Keepers, Losers Weepers*. Lippincott, 1967.

Low, Alice. *David's Windows*. Putnam, 1974.

MacLachlan, Patricia. *The Moon's Almost Here*. Simon & Schuster/McElderry Books, 2016.

MacLachlan, Patricia. *Moon, Stars, Frogs, and Friends*. Pantheon, 1980.

Madrigal, Antonio Hernández. *The Eagle and the Rainbow: Timeless Tales from Mexico*. Fulcrum, 1997.

Madrigal, Antonio Hernández. *Erandi's Braids*. Putnam, 1999.

McGovern, Ann. *Nicholas Bentley Stoningpot III*. Holiday House, 1982.

Miller, Lisa. *Sound*. Coward-McCann, 1965.

Miller, Lisa. *Wheels*. Coward-McCann, 1965.

Moore, Clement C. *The Night Before Christmas*. Holiday House, 1980.

Mooser, Stephen. *Funnyman and the Penny Dodo*. Franklin Watts, 1984.

Mooser, Stephen. *Funnyman's First Case*. Franklin Watts, 1981.

Mooser, Stephen. *The Ghost with the Halloween Hiccups*. Franklin Watts, 1977.

Murphy, Shirley Rousseau. *Tattie's River Journey*. Dial, 1983.

Norris, Kathleen. *The Holy Twins: Benedict and Scholastica*. Putnam, 2001.

O'Connor, Jane. *Benny's Big Bubble*. Grosset & Dunlap, 1997.

Oliver, Lin. *Little Poems for Tiny Ears*. Putnam, 2014.

Oliver, Lin. *Steppin' Out: Jaunty Rhymes for Playful Times*. Putnam, 2017.

Once upon a Time: A RIF Book, written and illustrated by Tomie dePaola et al. Putnam, 1986.

Pandell, Karen. *I Love You, Sun; I Love You, Moon*. Putnam, 1994.

Pinkwater, Daniel M. *The Wuggie Norple Story*. Four Winds Press, 1980.

Pitt, Valerie. *Let's Find Out About Communications*. Franklin Watts, 1973.

Prager, Annabelle. *The Spooky Halloween Party*. Pantheon, 1981.

Prager, Annabelle. *The Surprise Party*. Pantheon, 1977.

Rinkoff, Barbara. *Rutherford T. Finds 21B*. Putnam, 1970.

Rose, Anne. *The Triumphs of Fuzzy Fogtop*. Dial, 1979.

Saunders, Rubie. *The Franklin Watts Concise Guide to Baby-Sitting*. Franklin Watts, 1972.

Schneider, Nina. *Hercules, the Gentle Giant*. Hawthorn, 1969.

Shapiro, Arnold L. *Mice Squeak, We Speak*. Putnam, 1997.

Shapp, Martha and Charles. *Let's Find Out About Houses*. Franklin Watts, 1975.

Wahl, Jan. *Jamie's Tiger*. Harcourt Brace Jovanovich, 1978.

Wallace, Daisy, ed. *Ghost Poems*. Holiday House, 1979.

Ward, Cindy. *Cookie's Week*. Putnam, 1988.

Watson, Pauline. *The Walking Coat*. Walker, 1980.

Weiss, Malcolm E. *Solomon Grundy, Born on Oneday: A Finite Arithmetic Puzzle*. Crowell, 1977.

Willard, Nancy. *The Mountains of Quilt*. Harcourt Brace Jovanovich, 1987.

Willard, Nancy. *Simple Pictures Are Best*. Harcourt Brace Jovanovich, 1977.

Williams, Barbara. *If He's My Brother*. Harvey House, 1976.

Winthrop, Elizabeth. *Maggie and the Monster*. Holiday House, 1987.

Wise, William. *Monsters of the Middle Ages*. Putnam, 1971.

Yeomans, Thomas. *For Every Child a Star: A Christmas Story*. Holiday House, 1986.

Yolen, Jane. *The Giants' Farm*. Seabury Press, 1977.

Yolen, Jane. *The Giants Go Camping*. Seabury Press, 1979.

Yolen, Jane. *Hark! A Christmas Sampler*. Putnam, 1991.

Titles Written by Tomie dePaola, Illustrated by Others

Criss-Cross Applesauce. Illustrated by B. A. King and his children. Addison House, 1978.

In a Small Kingdom. Illustrated by Doug Salati. Simon & Schuster Books for Young Readers, 2018.

The Legend of the Persian Carpet. Illustrated by Claire Ewart. Putnam/Whitebird, 1993.

NOTE: DePaola's books have been translated into more than twenty-five languages.

Art Notes

The medium/media for the illustrations reproduced in this book is/are given after each title.

Andy & Sandy's Anything Adventure—acrylics with colored pencil
Andy & Sandy and the Big Talent Show—acrylics with colored pencil
Andy, That's My Name—three-color preseparated art
The Art Lesson—Rotring Artist Colors
The Baby Sister—Rotring Artist Colors
Big Anthony, His Story—Rotring Artist Colors
Bill and Pete—four-color preseparated art
Bill and Pete to the Rescue—transparent acrylics
The Birds of Bethlehem—opaque acrylics
Bonjour, Mr. Satie—acrylics
The Cat on the Dovrefell—acrylics
"Charlie Needs a Cloak"—three-color preseparated art
Christmas Remembered—acrylics and collage
Christopher, the Holy Giant—acrylics
The Clown of God—watercolors, colored inks, and pencil
Days of the Blackbird—acrylics
An Early American Christmas—Rotring Artist Colors and pencil
Fight the Night—two-color preseparated art
Fin M'Coul—Rotring Artist Colors and pencil
Francis, the Poor Man of Assisi—transparent colored inks
Guess Who's Coming to Santa's for Dinner?—acrylics
In a Small Kingdom—graphite and charcoal pencil, colored digitally
Jack—acrylics and rubber stamps
Jamie O'Rourke and the Pooka—acrylics
The Lady of Guadalupe—watercolors, colored inks, and pencil
The Legend of Old Befana—colored inks and watercolor
The Legend of the Bluebonnet—Rotring Artist Colors and tempera
Let the Whole Earth Sing Praise—transparent acrylics
Marianna May and Nursey—Rotring Artist Colors
Mary Had a Little Lamb—acrylics
Mary, the Mother of Jesus—acrylics
Merry Christmas, Strega Nona—pencil, transparent inks, and watercolor
Michael Bird-Boy—watercolor, colored pencil, and ink
Miracle on 34th Street—acrylics
The Moon's Almost Here—acrylics
The Mountains of Quilt—Rotring Artist Colors and colored pencils
Nana Upstairs & Nana Downstairs—three-color preseparated art

Nana Upstairs & Nana Downstairs, new edition—transparent acrylics

The Night before Christmas—watercolors and colored inks

Now One Foot, Now the Other—three-color preseparated art

Oliver Button Is a Sissy—three-color preseparated art

Patrick, Patron Saint of Ireland—acrylics

The Popcorn Book—three-color preseparated art

The Quicksand Book—three-color preseparated art

Quiet—transparent acrylics and colored pencil

The Quilt Story—acrylics

Sound—three-color preseparated art alternating with black and white

The Story of the Three Wise Kings—acrylics

Strega Nona—watercolors and pencil

Strega Nona and Her Tomatoes—acrylics with colored pencil

Strega Nona and the Twins—acrylics with colored pencil

Strega Nona, Her Story—Rotring Artist Colors and transparent acrylics

Strega Nona Takes a Vacation—acrylics

Strega Nona's Gift—transparent acrylics

Strega Nona's Harvest—transparent acrylics

Strega Nona's Magic Lessons—Rotring Artist Colors and transparent acrylics

Strega Nona's Magic Ring—Rotring Artist Colors and pencil

The Tale of Rabbit and Coyote—acrylics

Tom—transparent acrylics

Tomie dePaola's Favorite Nursery Tales—transparent acrylics

Tomie dePaola's Front Porch Tales & North Country Whoppers—acrylics

Tomie dePaola's Mother Goose—transparent acrylics

26 Fairmount Avenue—black line and wash

Wheels—three-color preseparated art alternating with black and white

Wings—collage using Avery full-sheet labels with markers for the color; background paper was painted using acrylics

Art and Photo Credits

For their willingness to grant permission to reprint images from Tomie dePaola's books, grateful acknowledgment is given here to the following publishers:

Holiday House

Christopher, the Holy Giant. Copyright © 1994 by Tomie dePaola.

An Early American Christmas. Copyright © 1987 by Tomie dePaola.

Fin M'Coul: The Giant of Knockmany Hill. Copyright © 1981 by Tomie dePaola.

Francis, the Poor Man of Assisi. Copyright © 1982 by Tomie dePaola.

The Lady of Guadalupe. Copyright © 1980 by Tomie dePaola.

Mary Had a Little Lamb by Sarah Josepha Hale. Illustrations copyright © 1984 by Tomie dePaola.

Mary, the Mother of Jesus. Copyright © 1995 by Tomie dePaola.

The Night Before Christmas by Clement C. Moore. Illustrations copyright © 1980 by Tomie dePaola.

Patrick, Patron Saint of Ireland. Copyright © 1992 by Tomie dePaola.

The Popcorn Book. Copyright © 1978 by Tomie dePaola.

The Quicksand Book. Copyright © 1977 by Tomie dePaola.

Houghton Mifflin Harcourt

The Mountains of Quilt by Nancy Willard. Illustrations copyright © 1987 by Tomie dePaola.

Penguin Random House
DIAL BOOKS FOR YOUNG READERS

The Triumphs of Fuzzy Fogtop by Anne Rose. Illustrations copyright © 1979 by Tomie dePaola

G. P. PUTNAM'S SONS

The Art Lesson. Copyright © 1989 by Tomie dePaola.

The Baby Sister. Copyright © 1996 by Tomie dePaola.

Big Anthony, His Story. Copyright © 1998 by Tomie dePaola.

Bill and Pete. Copyright © 1978 by Tomie dePaola.

Bill and Pete to the Rescue. Copyright © 1998 by Tomie dePaola.

Bonjour, Mr. Satie. Copyright © 1991 by Tomie dePaola.

Days of the Blackbird. Copyright © 1997 by Tomie dePaola.

Jamie O'Rourke and the Pooka. Copyright © 2000 by Tomie dePaola.

The Legend of the Bluebonnet. Copyright © 1983 by Tomie dePaola.

Let the Whole Earth Sing Praise. Copyright © 2011 by Tomie dePaola.

Nana Upstairs & Nana Downstairs. Copyright © 1973, 1998 by Tomie dePaola.

Now One Foot, Now the Other. Copyright © 1981 by Tomie dePaola.

The Quilt Story by Tony Johnston. Illustrations copyright © 1985 by Tomie dePaola.

Sound by Lisa Miller. Illustrations copyright © 1965 by Tomie dePaola.

Strega Nona, Her Story. Copyright © 1996.

Strega Nona Takes a Vacation. Copyright © 2000 by Tomie dePaola.

Strega Nona's Harvest. Copyright © 2009 by Tomie dePaola.

The Tale of Rabbit and Coyote by Tony Johnston. Illustrations copyright © 1994 by Tomie dePaola.

Tom. Copyright © 1993 by Tomie dePaola.

Tomie dePaola's Favorite Nursery Tales. Illustrations copyright © 1986 by Tomie dePaola.

Tomie dePaola's Front Porch Tales & North Country Whoppers. Copyright © 2007 by Tomie dePaola.

Tomie dePaola's Mother Goose. Illustrations copyright © 1985 by Tomie dePaola.

26 Fairmount Avenue. Copyright © 1999 by Tomie dePaola.

Wheels by Lisa Miller. Illustrations copyright © 1965 by Tomie dePaola.

NANCY PAULSEN BOOKS

The Birds of Bethlehem. Copyright © 2012 by Tomie dePaola.

Jack. Copyright © 2014 by Tomie dePaola.

The Magical World of Strega Nona: A Treasury. Copyright © 2015 by Tomie dePaola.

Strega Nona's Gift. Copyright © 2011 by Tomie dePaola.

Simon & Schuster Books for Young Readers

Andy & Sandy and the Big Talent Show. Illustrations copyright © 2017 by Tomie dePaola.

Andy & Sandy's Anything Adventure. Illustrations copyright © 2016 by Tomie dePaola.

Andy, That's My Name. Copyright © 1973 by Tomie dePaola.

The Cat on the Dovrefell. Text copyright © 2021 by Tomie dePaola. Illustrations copyright © 1979 by Tomie dePaola.

"Charlie Needs a Cloak." Copyright © 1973 by Tomie dePaola.

The Clown of God. Copyright © 1978 by Tomie dePaola.

The Comic Adventures of Old Mother Hubbard and Her Dog. Copyright © 1981 by Tomie dePaola.

Fight the Night. Copyright © 1968, renewed 1996 by Tomie dePaola.

Guess Who's Coming to Santa's for Dinner? Copyright © 2004 by Tomie dePaola.

In a Small Kingdom by Tomie dePaola. Illustrations © 2018 by Douglas Steele Salati.

The Legend of Old Befana. Copyright © 1980 by Tomie dePaola.

Marianna May and Nursey. Copyright © 1983 by Tomie dePaola.

Michael Bird-Boy. Copyright © 1975 by Tomie dePaola.

The Moon's Almost Here by Patricia MacLachlan. Illustrations copyright © 2016 by Tomie dePaola.

Oliver Button Is a Sissy. Copyright © 1979 by Tomie dePaola.

Quiet. Copyright © 2018 by Tomie dePaola.

The Story of the Three Wise Kings. Copyright © 1983 by Tomie dePaola.

Strega Nona. Copyright © 1975 by Tomie dePaola.

Strega Nona and Her Tomatoes. Copyright © 2017 by Tomie dePaola.

Strega Nona's Magic Lessons. Copyright © 1982 by Tomie dePaola.

Strega Nona's Magic Ring. Copyright © 1979 by Tomie dePaola.

Strega Nona and the Twins. Copyright © 2017 by Tomie dePaola.

Wings by Cheryl B. Klein. Illustrations copyright © 2019 by Tomie dePaola.

ADDITIONAL THANKS TO:

The Children's Book Council, New York, New York, for photo on page 119.

Stephanie Clayton, for photo on page 172.

Laurent Linn, for photos on pages 8, 9, 10 (top), 18, 21, 24–25, 26, 28, 81, 86, 92, 105, 117, 133, 167, and 169.

All other photos are from the author or from dePaola's personal collection.

UNCAPTIONED ILLUSTRATIONS

page ii: *The Clown of God*

page iii: *The Clown of God*

page iv: *The Legend of Old Befana*

page v: *Andy, That's My Name*

page vi: *The Clown of God*

page 3: *Quiet*

page 4: *Wings*

page 7, top: *Quiet*

page 7, bottom: self-portrait by dePaola

page 9: *Quiet*

page 11: *Quiet*

page 13: *Strega Nona*

page 20: *Strega Nona*

page 29: *Oliver Button Is a Sissy*

page 30: *Andy, That's My Name*

page 32: *Andy, That's My Name*

page 47: line drawing of Strega Nona by dePaola

page 55, top: *Days of the Blackbird*

page 57: *Days of the Blackbird*

page 65, top and bottom: *The Story of the Three Wise Kings*

page 66, bottom: *The Lady of Guadalupe*

page 70, bottom: *The Story of the Three Wise Kings*

page 75, bottom: *The Clown of God*

page 79, top: *Guess Who's Coming to Santa's for Dinner?*

page 82, bottom: *Guess Who's Coming to Santa's for Dinner?*

page 89: *Strega Nona*

page 91, top: *Tomie dePaola's Mother Goose*

page 91, bottom: *The Clown of God*

page 95: *The Legend of Old Befana*

page 99, top: *The Legend of Old Befana*

page 109, top: *The Comic Adventures of Old Mother Hubbard and Her Dog*

page 120, bottom: *The Story of the Three Wise Kings*

page 125: *The Lady of Guadalupe*

page 126: *Francis, the Poor Man of Assisi*

page 129, top: *Quiet*

page 129, bottom: *Strega Nona*

page 130, bottom: line drawing of Strega Nona from the *Strega Nona* 40th anniversary edition case cover

page 132: *Strega Nona*

page 139: *Quiet*

page 141: *Quiet*

page 147, top: *Pears Triptych*

Index

Books and works written and/or illustrated by Tomie dePaola are indicated by an asterisk (*).
Illustrations and photographs are denoted by page numbers in *italics.*.